D0298392

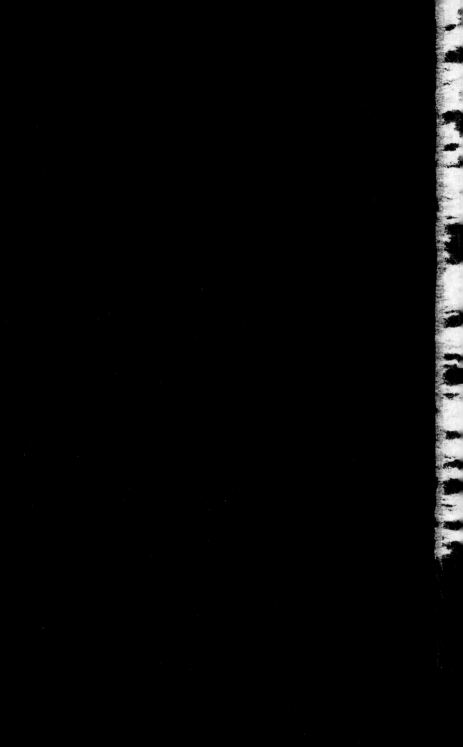

Boulting's Vélosaurus

Also by Ned Boulting

How I Won the Yellow Jumper
How Cav Won the Green Jersey
On the Road Bike
101 Damnations

NED BOULTING

Boulting's Vélosaurus

A Linguistic Tour de France

YELLOW JERSEY PRESS
LONDON

1 3 5 7 9 10 8 6 4 2

Yellow Jersey Press, an imprint of Vintage
20 Vauxhall Bridge Road
London SW1V 2SA

Yellow Jersey Press is part of the Penguin Random House group of companies
whose addresses can be found at global.penguinrandomhouse.com

Copyright © Ned Boulting 2016
Illustrations copyright © Robbie Porter

Ned Boulting has asserted his right to be identified as the author of this Work
in accordance with the Copyright, Designs and Patents Act 1988

First published by Yellow Jersey Press in 2016

penguin.co.uk/vintage

A CIP catalogue record for this book is available from the British Library

ISBN 9780224100649

Typeset in 10.75/13.25 pt Adobe Caslon
by Jouve (UK), Milton Keynes
Printed and bound by Clays Ltd, St Ives plc

To Rob Llewelyn,
Remembering all the shared Julys.

Chapeau! (Hat!)

Congratulations on buying this book. If you don't like it, Uncle Clive might.

The language of the *peloton* is rich, fascinating, and terrifyingly French. Cycling cognoscenti casually refer to the *échappée* and talk of *rouleurs* and *pavé*, leaving outsiders nodding sagely in a fog of incomprehension.

Well, bluff no more!

My Vélosaurus is designed to immerse you in the complex code and culture of French bicycling language, a hidden world of arcane meaning, featuring a wealth of more or less trustworthy curiosities from a hundred years of meticulously researched history. It is a treasure trove of French cycling vocabulary designed to expand your horizons to breaking point. And probably beyond.

Today is the *Grand Départ* of your *Éducation Cycliste*.

Prepare to be enlightened.

Allez. (Go on, then . . .)

Paris, 24 July 2016

Alpe *nm*

An Alp.

A

Accroissement (marginal) *nm*

A (marginal) gain.

This much-lauded ethos of Team Sky (see *Ciel*) has become part of mainstream cycling culture, with riders looking for all sorts of implausible ways to seek out any kind of advantage over their peers, however infinitesimal. But it should be noted that the guiding principle of the *accroissement* philosophy has not always been understood and enacted with total coherence in French cycling culture.

In 2013, the *directeur sportif* of the little-known Laverie La Poste-Yogadrome team from Brest, Yann Pleyber, changed all the mobile phone numbers of his riders to palindromic numbers.

It was his curious, and perhaps misguided, belief that the numbers would be easier to memorise if they were constructed along a central line of lateral symmetry. This, in turn, would foster a greater tendency for his charges to call and text each other. Such increased communication, in itself, would lead to marginally greater levels of team bonding, an effect that would play itself out to their advantage in the upcoming team time trial in the Tour du Finistère.

Pleyber estimated that this change in the telephone numbers of his cohort would ultimately be worth 2.25 seconds.

As it happened, the results were inconclusive, at best. Laverie La Poste-Yogadrome finished eleventh in the team time trial, and started the race a man short.

Their missing teammate claimed that no one had sent him a text message about the start time, and he turned up twenty minutes late.

Ajustage *nm*

Faffing.

An obsession with effecting tiny adjustments to the height of the seat post, the angle of the handlebars and the tightness of the straps on one's shoes.

This practice divides cycling opinion right down the middle. In some teams, most notably the Russian outfit Katusha, *ajustage* is frowned upon, and riders found guilty of such a charge are routinely punished by having to gargle a cup of chain lube and sing a Gregorian chant.

Whereas in other cultures, specifically Italian, a ludicrous attention to detail and relentless dissatisfaction with the set-up of one's bike is considered a virtue.

Riders' contracts often include a bonus clause for *ajustage*, thus ensuring that, at winter training camps in particular, the rides often start over two hours late, such is the degree of unbridled fettling and tape-measure work outside the hotel before they set off. It is generally understood within Italian teams that it is in no one's interests to speed this process up.

Ambulatoire *adj*

Bruising. Worthy of the deployment of an ambulance.

A race is considered to be *ambulatoire* if it displays any of the following features, all of which increase the chances that a rider will be leaving in the back of an ambulance: cobbles, rain, wind, cobbles.

The infamous Paris–Roubaix, of course, normally contains all four of these hazards, but is, for some reason, romanticised for its sheer dangerousness. It is the ultimate *course ambulatoire* and is celebrated as such by tens of thousands of cycling fans who make their way to the side of the road in the specific hope of taking a selfie with a badly injured rider as he lies face first in a puddle.

In fact, in 1974, the Hornby cycling toy range featured a special edition commemorative Paris–Roubaix set, complete with a two-foot length of recessed cobblestones (see *Pavé*), tin figures of drunken Flemish and French fans (two of whom are engaged in a fist fight), manure transfers with which to decorate the road and a Citroën ambulance van in French livery, whose rear doors open to reveal a stricken Eddy Merckx, clutching his collar bone and screaming in pain.

Such sets are extremely collectable and routinely fetch prices in the region of £11–11.75 on eBay.

Not to be confused with *andouillette*.

Anchois *nm*

An unwanted addition to a race, such as a sharp climb in the final five hundred metres. Like an anchovy (*anchois*) on a pizza, it is an unnecessary and ruinous elaboration on an otherwise trustworthy format.

Andouillette *nf*

A surprisingly grisly cycling event.

Named after the eponymous tripe-based sausage, often mistakenly ordered by foreign tourists in French restaurants when trying to bluff their way through the menu, this term describes any race that turns out to be unexpectedly unpleasant.

The first, and to this date only, Tour of the Caucasus is often believed to be the ultimate *andouillette*, featuring as it did in 2008 long flat stages, through grizzled suburbs of war-torn cities, with little or no crowd save for the occasional three-legged, scavenging dog and a procession of Russian partisans passing in the opposite direction in the back of pick-up trucks.

This view of the race was common currency. The continuing bad press it received and the litany of very public complaints from riders about the conditions at the event prompted the organisers to respond.

They posted the following infamous outburst on their Facebook page as a reaction to the growing complaints from the cycling community: 'What do you expect? Caviar? Haven't any of you read Bertolt Brecht? The clue's in the name! Of course it's an *andouillette*.'

This is still believed to be the only recorded link between the works of Brecht and professional cycling, except for the recently released Italian documentary, *The Resistible Rise of Vincenzo Nibali*.

Angers *adj*

Past caring.

Pertaining to, or descriptive of, the state of bewildered ennui to which riders and the rest of the entourage succumb during the middle week of a Grand Tour.

It is generally accepted that from Stage Seven onwards no one involved in the race has the faintest idea where they are, where they were the day before, nor where they will be the following day. It is because no one actually knows with any degree of exactitude where the French town of Angers is that this most humble of conurbations has become synonymous with a state of ingrained confusion, e.g. 'Where are we tomorrow?' 'I don't know . . . *Angers*?'*

Moreover, its usage has further been developed to describe a mental state of indifference and lethargy. 'Ça va?', you might enquire of a colleague over coffee in the morning. 'Un peu *Angers*' might be the response, accompanied by a deeply affected shrug and a thousand-yard stare out of the window.

Animateur *nm*

Any team bus driver who enlivens a fairly dull stage by crashing into the finishing arch and getting his vehicle stuck (see *Orica*).

Arithméticien *nm*

An irritating rider, preoccupied with the number of kilometres remaining, and unable to keep the information to himself.

---

* Because of these negative connotations, the municipality of Angers has long battled to free itself of such associations. After consultation with the British town of Scunthorpe, which itself has fought hard to improve its image in the public consciousness, Angers launched an aggressive rebranding campaign to coincide with its status as Ville d'arrivée for Stage Six of the 2004 Tour de France. Under the motto 'Don't Worry, Be Angers', it handed out thousands of multi-coloured wigs, which it hoped would be worn by the enthusiastic crowds for the benefit of a huge worldwide television audience.

Arlequin *nm*

A ludicrously clad rider.

A professional cyclist forced to wear a comically ugly team kit, patterned with chevrons, checks and/or primary colours. Anyone who has ever ridden for AG2R La Mondiale.

Arriviste *nmf*

A rider who times his or her effort to perfection, arriving with uncanny precision and at the very last minute to take the victory, having been entirely invisible for the preceding hundreds of kilometres and having contributed nothing to the chase.

Arrivistes are generally deeply unpopular figures in the *peloton*, and are known to be loners, shunned at the breakfast table and forced to eat dinner on their own, often with sputum in their pasta, seasoned secretly in the kitchens by their teammates. However, historically they are the best-paid riders in the team, since they win the most races. This does nothing to add to their popularity. As such, the word itself has become a totem for unpleasant characteristics: avarice, selfishness, deviousness, ruthlessness.

Its use has spread beyond cycling into literature. In 1963, the absurdist Romanian poet and former winner of the Tour of Transylvania Gheorghe Zimbrean, writing from exile in Paris, adopted the expression when he published his seminal collection *Moi? Arriviste. Toi? Penis*, a free-form poetic rhapsody in celebration of cycling. And genitals.

Astronaute *nm*

Lance Armstrong.

Having not won the Tour de France seven times, the Texan rider then went on to claim that he, and not his namesake Neil, had in fact been the first man on the moon.

Athée *nmf*

One who does not believe in God.

A term usually applied to either journalist David Walsh or Paul Kimmage.

This was a phrase originally coined by Lance Armstrong (see *Astronaute*) during his valedictory Tour (before his valedictory comeback) in 2005. After his famous farewell speech on the Champs-Élysées, in which he claimed to pity those who 'don't believe in miracles', he then went on to claim that he was bigger than The Beatles.*

Attiser *vtr*

To wind-up, gob-off, sledge or generally 'give it some verbals' in the bunch.

---

* Armstrong is currently being pursued in court for damages in a joint civil action by Sir Paul McCartney, the Dalai Lama and His Holiness Pope Francis.

Australian riders, it is generally acknowledged, are seen to have imported the habit of *attisement* to the European cycling scene in the late 1980s, starting with Phil Anderson, who used to own a truly horrid joke about a man's nose.

The most infamous exponent of the dark art in recent times is Tasmania's diminutive climber Richie Porte, a man in possession of a jibe so unpleasant that it needs to be kept locked up in the hotel safe every night in case it escapes. It is believed to relate in some way to salad cream (see *Badinage*).

Aubade [Campanile] *nf*

A rude call to arms.

The dawn serenade of the Campanile hotel, a chain favoured (for purely financial reasons) by teams competing in continental bike races.

Whilst the unwelcome and over-early *aubade* is associated, if not uniquely, then frequently with Campaniles, the nature of the unprompted wake-up call may vary greatly.

Traditionally, and especially if you are staying anywhere near Tours, Rouen or Macon, this noisy interruption to your sleep will take the form of building work starting outside the window at an unreasonable hour. But an alarm going off and being ignored in the room next door, someone's bladder giving out and a rush for the toilet in the room above or a riotous fart from a roommate will have the same effect. A return to sleep is rendered impossible by the need to get straight on to

Twitter to complain about the fact that you have just been woken up. Often used in conjunction with expletives, a hashtag (#AubadeCampanile) and a bedraggled selfie.

Autoguidage *nm*

Racing by remote control.

A recently coined term, principally conceived to describe the racing tactics employed by Team Sky (see *Ciel*).

During the 2012 and 2013 seasons, rumours spread like wildfire through the *peloton* that Sky had begun an ambitious programme of micro-lobotomies. It was said that, in an effort to reduce the uncontrollable effects of independent thought, thus impairing their riders' capacity for doing what they were told, the team had identified a troublesome cluster of synapses in the lower temporal lobe, associated with having one's own opinions about stuff.

Overseen by Sir Dave Brailsford, with input from the brilliant psychologist Steve Peters, this highly secretive project was driven forward by a Canadian trepanist called Akkituyok (an Inuit name meaning 'dear' or 'expensive').

An investigative report by David Walsh (see *Athé*) in the *Sunday Times* revealed that Brailsford had first got to know the Canadian when he was embedded with the mounted police during the winter of 2008 on a clandestine fact-finding mission to see if there was 'anything cycling could learn from the world of equestrian law-enforcement in extremely hostile environments'.

Autopsie *nf*

An uncomfortable inquiry.

The forensic dissection of a rider's failed attempt to complete a race, conducted under duress, and carried out by a quietly furious sports director (see *Directeur sportif*) shortly after the rider has climbed into his team car (see *Corbillard*) and abandoned.

Avocat *nm*

A term with a dual meaning.

For the French-speaking cycling world, it refers to a rider with a strong sense of justice and an in-depth working knowledge of the rules and regulations governing all aspects of the sport.

For riders from the USA, the UK and Australia it simply means an avocado pear.

Brontosaure *nm*

A lumbering, slow-moving, vegetarian rider. (Obsolete.)

B

Babiller *vi*

To ride incoherently and without a plan, as if one has not the faintest idea what one is doing.

The most infamous *babilleur* of the mid 1980s was the Parisian rider Guy Parfouffe, the son of a chocolatier from the salubrious suburb of Neuilly-sur-Seine.

Parfouffe, a rangy figure with a huge beaked nose and a marked lisp, counted the music of difficult-to-listen-to German composer Stockhausen amongst his passions, along with an appreciation of falconry imagery in French Medieval poetry. An aesthete through and through, he was, by his own sometimes tearful admission, so uncomfortable in the coarse hurly-burly of the contemporary *peloton* that he would frequently feature in the breakaway, or at least try to, simply to get away from all the *badinage*, not to mention the *attisement*.

This he did with impulsive abandon, attacking whenever the road turned left, went uphill, turned right or ran over a level crossing. In fact, so predictable were his wild and ultimately doomed attempts to get away on his own, that the bunch would often funnel over to the left-hand side of the road to allow him the passage to launch his over-exuberant attack, waving him forward with impatient gestures and rather rude insults.

Parfouffe always obliged, nose down and avoiding eye contact, legs spinning wildly.

As a result of his trademark and completely pointless attacks, the 'Prix Parfouffe' became a fixture of French TV coverage of the Tour. During a long stretch in the 1990s, it was awarded on a daily basis to the rider who had displayed the highest level of *babillage*.

Parfouffe himself never won the prize.

Bactériologiste *nmf*

A rider who knows of a cure to almost any illness and will not hesitate for a second in offering advice to a stricken rider, whether solicited or not.

A *bactériologiste* will also undoubtedly have suffered from said complaint. In fact, they'll have had it more frequently, more acutely and with more uncontrollable itching than you.

Badinage *nm*

Ribald, amusing conversation, aimed at effecting team spirit through ritual humiliation.

In the Anglophone *peloton* (see *Super*), such boisterous hilarity is known simply as 'banter' or even 'bantz', and has been perfected into something of an art form by Team Sky's Welsh star Geraint Thomas, whose dry wit and lively sense of teasing fun has been known on occasion to stray into *attisement*.

However, banter's French cousin *badinage* is considerably more sophisticated, and likely to feature literary allusions.

For example, the recently retired Jérome Pineau was a master of *badinage*; his jokes often alluded with great wit and elegance to masterpieces of the nineteenth-century French canon.

Pineau was once overheard at breakfast ridiculing his teammate Sylvain Chavanel for his 'excessive use of pomade, as if he were trying to seduce Madame Bovary herself', referring to the heroine of the eponymous novel by Gustave Flaubert, who hailed from the same region in which the former French time-trial champion had first signed for a professional team.

Pineau's wonderfully phrased quip was greeted by a wave of appreciative chuckles from his IAM Cycling teammates, all of whom, at that time, had signed up to a correspondence course in the Tradition of the Novella from the University of Nottingham.

For the record, Chavanel ignored him and poured himself a coffee.

Bagatelle *nf*

(i) A derisory financial offer, made by a weaker, yet richer opponent to 'buy' a race from a stronger, poorer rival.
(ii) The media 'mixed-zone' behind the podium of the Tour de France, through which the riders must pass, bouncing from microphone to microphone like a ball on a bagatelle board.
(iii) The Tour of Britain.

Bailli *nm*

A bailiff, or debt collector. A rider with a long memory for outstanding favours that should be repaid, often years after the event.

A seeming lack of gratitude for a good deed done can quickly become the source of festering resentment within the closeted world of the *peloton*. Some riders have become famous for their sense of grievance, which they have been known to turn into a form of currency.

The Belgian *rouleur* Kevin Sandrijder would routinely 'gift' other riders virtually irrelevant bonus seconds at intermediate sprints on meaningless stages of unimportant races, in the knowledge that he could exploit this perceived generosity in the future.

Years later, he would expect these favours to be returned, but with considerable added interest. In a tearful radio interview broadcast just after his retirement, Andy Schleck recounted how his entire career had been blighted by the obligation he felt towards Sandrijder and his team of *baillis*. This indebtedness came about as a result of Sandrijder lending Schleck his pump in 2009 on a training ride. It was a gesture with consequences for Schleck, as well as for Sandrijder's closest friend in the *peloton*, Alberto Contador, who was the best man at Sandrijder's wedding to Contador's sister.

In 2010, still conscious that the loan of his pump had not been recompensed, Sandrijder called in the debt.

'I wouldn't have minded too much,' recalled Schleck in 2013, 'had it stopped at me being forced to gift Alberto Contador the 2010 Tour de France. But one day, Sandrijder's brothers turned up outside my house in Luxembourg and demanded the telly. And my sandwich toaster.'

Bakélite *nf*

An imposter, a phoney leader, a rider in a falsely elevated position.

The origins of this word are obscure, but it is widely thought to refer both to Bakelite, the brittle forerunner of plastic, and Jan Bakelants, the Belgian opportunist who snuck into an unexpected yellow jersey on the 2013 Tour.

Since his subsequent and quite inevitable surrender of the race lead, the expression 'c'est de la *Bakélite*' has become common parlance.

Bakelants has tried to distance himself from the phrase by telling everyone he hears using it to 'flikker op'.

Banjo *nm*

A pejorative term to denote a massively annoying rider.

This phrase was first coined by Eddy Merckx in 1972, shortly after the release of the film *Deliverance*, which featured the famous 'duelling banjos' sequence in which a strange inbred delinquent reveals himself to have astonishing virtuosity at the banjo.

Likening his sometime rival, the Spanish climber Benjamin Garcia Carrion, to the character of Lonnie from the film, Merckx was quoted as asking with incredulity: 'Is Carrion really to be spoken of as my equal? Yes, if the banjo is the equal of a full orchestra.'

This comment came after a series of mountaintop finishes in the Tour of Catalonia in which the taciturn Spaniard clung to Merckx's wheel, proving annoyingly unshakeable.

Responding some days later to Merckx's dismissive description of his tactics, Carrion replied in an interview with *La Marca* that 'A banjo is a noble and resolute instrument, capable of great expression. If Señor Merckx has not the humility to see that even the humblest of organs can produce wonders, then he has no place pontificating from on high. To me, he is nothing so grand,' Carrion continued. 'To me, he is simply a coarse bassoon. Or maybe a euphonium.'

Carrion died in penury in 1995, and a simple headstone bearing the symbol of a banjo marks his grave. The stone was a gift of the Merckx family.

Bassiste *nmf*

A silent, unheralded, often lugubrious rider, whose function within the team is simply to perform the same tiresomely repetitive tasks over and over again, in a certain dreadful rhythm.

Baudelairien *adj*

An adjective used to describe a particularly flowery race report in *L'Équipe*. Pejorative.

Baver *vi*

Literally, to dribble, slobber or drool.

This verb is closely associated with, and is in many ways a slight precursor to, the American English expression 'to bonk', describing collapsing with exhaustion induced by hunger and thirst.

The empty feeling that can overwhelm a cyclist must be warded off at all costs, often by the forced feeding of bananas, flapjacks, horrible little buns, sandwiches, crisps, Cornish pasties and roast pork, all of which are pulled from the rear pockets of riders on the move.

Certain riders (*baveurs*) develop a reputation for unabashed and continual feeding, starting at the breakfast table, continuing on the bus to the start, during the race, through the finish line, onto the bus to the hotel and straight to the dinner table. They are not popular and tend to sit in isolation, chomping and slavering, wide-eyed and desperate, as their colleagues whisper about them in disgust. 'Regarde Alain. Il *bave* encore, le cochon.'

The most notorious *baveur* of all time, according to legend, was the Danish sprinter Willy Lars Ankerman, who, fearing the 'bonk', once stole a Camembert baguette from a child on the slopes of the Col d'Aspin on the 1964 Tour. He was subsequently arrested by gendarmes that evening at his hotel in Lourdes, after a complaint was made by the child's father.

Ankerman, a socialist, confessed all at the police station, to the satisfaction of the boy's father, a fervent Catholic, who agreed to drop the charges on condition that Ankerman visit the Sanctuary of Our Lady of Lourdes the following morning before the stage start and pray aloud for forgiveness, with the entire *peloton* of the Tour de France as witnesses.

Blanchâtre *adj*

Dodgy.

Literally, whitish or off-white. *Blanchâtre* has become shorthand for the expression of doubt as to the propriety of any given rider. It takes its origins from the hue and tint of post-race, or indeed out-of-competition, doping tests.

Urine, as passed by the Innocent, even given the extreme dehydration resulting from a stage of the Tour de France, should smell pure, glisten translucently and seduce with its sparkle. It should have the aroma of freshly cut grass and resemble alcohol-free Absolut vodka. The slightest trace of non-white, impure contaminants will lead inevitably to nasty rumour-mongering that the donor was himself *blanchâtre* or 'not exactly right' or 'a wrong-un' or, in extremis, *Vinokourov*.

Riders who have been revealed to be *blanchâtre* are faced with a bleak choice. They can either protest their innocence, refuse to talk about it, and proceed pretty much unimpeded with their career. Or they can confess to their guilt, become a 'spokesman', publish a book and proceed pretty much unimpeded with their career.

Either way, the general public will never really know the truth. (See *Urologie*.)

Bouif *nm*

A cobbler.

A *bouif* is a term used widely in France to describe an old-school cyclist, who demonstrates an almost post-war attitude towards 'making-do and mending'.

The most celebrated *bouif* in the *peloton* was Claude Rimbaud, a *rouleur* from Normandy, who was born into a parsimonious church family. His father had spent protracted periods of time serving as a missionary in Indochina, where life had been hard and raw materials scarce. As a result, he had imbued his son with a hatred for wastage, and breathtaking ingenuity.

Thus, no one was particularly surprised when, during an attritional edition of Paris–Tours in 1953, Rimbaud's saddle came loose and fell off, and the resourceful Frenchman managed to finish the race seated atop a turnip.

He had pulled one from the ground in an adjacent field (see *Échalote*), quickly dug a central hole out with his Allen key, and planted it onto his seat tube. It offered just enough protection for Rimbaud to make his way to the finish line some 20 kilometres away, gingerly perched on the root vegetable.

To this day, the 1953 Paris–Tours is remembered as 'La Course du Navet'; literally, 'The Race of the Turnip'.

Britannique *adj*

Infernally arrogant. Probably doping.

Brocante *nf*

A second-hand, or junk shop.

The name given to an informal online black market within the lower ranks of the professional scene, through which bits and pieces of team-issue kit and clothing find their way onto the open market in order to supplement riders' meagre income.

Brucelles *nfpl*

Tweezers.

The deceptively underdeveloped legs of a physically unimpressive first-year professional; small twig-like limbs, much like tweezers, that nonetheless can inflict great pain and suffering when used to the full extent of their function.

A young Eddy Merckx, on his first appearance in the Belgian Junior National Road Race Championships, was nicknamed 'Les *Brucelles* de Bruxelles' by the Belgian daily *Le Soir* after he lapped the field with 60 kilometres still left to ride.

To this day, and in his honour, the newspaper still awards the annual 'Prix *Brucelles*' to the young rider with the most surprising power in his inauspicious, scarcely mature legs. The winner receives a pair of golden tweezers in a presentation case and a cheque for €100.

The prize was briefly sponsored by Belgian cosmetics giant Polyflirt.

Chameau *nm*

A camel, or a rider who never, or at least very seldom, succumbs to the urge to urinate. (See *Pistolet* (*à eau*).)

C

Capilliculteur *nm*

An extravagantly coiffed rider.

The first rider to accede to this title was the flamboyantly hir-sute Florent Pelouse, the winner of La Flèche Wallonne in 1937. A Saint Petersburg-educated dandy, recently returned from his travels in the Far East, during which he penned a famous discursive poem 'L'Amour et les Cheveux' ('Love and Hair'), Pelouse made an instant impact amongst the chattering classes of Parisian society – not the most natural constituency for cycling personalities. This curiously ardent admiration was principally due to his flowing locks which, teased from 'neath his cap, billowed artfully down to his waist. For a while, the 'Pelouse' was a fashionable haircut on the Rive Gauche.

Most *capilliculteurs* of the 1980s and 1990s (most notably, of course, Laurent Brochard) sported the mullet, until it was banned by the Union Cycliste Internationale (UCI) in 2001.

In more recent times, German sprinter Marcel Kittel has taken up the mantel, aided in no small part by having ridden for a team sponsored by a German caffeine-based shampoo, prompting the latest edition of the *Duden Deutsches Wörterbuch* to include the newly acknowledged term 'Der Kapillikulturismus', meaning 'undue attention to the maintenance of an excessively groomed mane'.

Caque *nf*

Literally, a 'herring barrel'.

The regimented and predictable way in which the races of the early nineties were conducted.

This phrase was first coined by the notorious, outspoken French television commentator Christophe Marmite during live coverage of the 1993 Tour de France. It turned out to be a race of such stupendous tedium that few people can remember its outcome, including its eventual winner Miguel Indurain, who refuses to talk about it to this day.

Caque's first usage can be traced to Stage Three, when during a typically dull phase of a particularly pointless, predictable and flat race, Marmite was asked by his fellow commentator what he thought of the modern *peloton*.

'C'est une *caque*,' he replied, without hesitation.

When asked to explain his rather strange analogy, he offered up the following reasoning, which has gone down in broadcasting folklore.

'It's because every rider in the bunch is a slithering, stinking, unlovely beast, rubbing itself against its nearest neighbour and wriggling through his miserable existence like the base life-form that he is.'

After a brief moment during which he allowed that to sink in, he then continued, in an extraordinary broadside aimed at a pair of unexpected targets.

'No one likes herrings, except the Norwegians. And who gives the slightest shit what they think about anything, the oil-rich barbarians. Fuck them, and fuck the Tour de France.'

There was a slight pause in the broadcast, before his co-host then uttered the now famous words, 'we'll be back after a short break'.

Cascadeur *nm*

A stuntman.

Some riders decide that they will never amount to very much. This normally happens at the midway point in their career when they are experiencing a moment of *judgement*, the point at which they understand that they are destined merely to make up the numbers. As a result of this chastening awakening to their mediocrity, some of these will take an active, if tacit, decision to become a *cascadeur*.

This can be humbling. But it can also be quite lucrative.

A good *cascadeur* is worth his weight in gold for the team's sponsors. For example, in 2001, when Willy Neff quite deliberately hit a pothole, flew over a barbed-wire fence, and landed atop a Friesian dairy cow in a field near Morlaix, the image of his impromptu bovine embrace was wired around the world within minutes and gave the otherwise anonymous Brill Cooking Utensils Team millions of pounds worth of free exposure. In a few days, Neff's contract had been renewed, and Brill had sold out of egg whisks and were running short on mixing bowls.

It was only a week later, when a Breton villager sold his story to *L'Équipe*, that the 'Affaire Neff' started to look a little less wholesome. The local claimed that he had spotted Neff one week before the Tour de France, digging a hole in the tarmac and repeatedly practising his dismount using a vaulting horse as a makeshift cow. On the morning of the stage itself, he had also photographed Neff's brother leading a Friesian into the field and pinning its hooves to a pre-marked spot on the ground with tent pegs and twine.

Chaise (électrique) *nf*

An obviously motor-doped bicycle; one that will almost certainly be discovered. With wires sticking out.

Ciel *nm*

Sky.

Colombien *adj*

A Colombian.

Relating to any mysterious, pint-sized and largely unsmiling climber whose biography is broadly unknown, but presumed to be of Colombian peasant stock.

Since no one ever really bothers to ask them, it is conveniently assumed that *colombiens* are universally conditioned to excel in the mountains, given a childhood characterised by daily twenty-hour rides to and from school over 6,000-metre Andean passes. The fact that, inconveniently, some of them grew up at sea level seems to matter not a jot.

It is customary for more traditionally minded European teams to buy two *colombiens*. It is believed that they work better as a pair, like hamsters. Or the Gallagher brothers.

Providing *colombiens* with a friend from home avoids the need for their more culturally sophisticated European riders to mix socially with their South American colleagues, who will simply be grateful for the opportunity to race on The Old Continent and share a room, mobile phone and a seat at the back of the bus with their little pal from Colombia.

Commisération *nf*

An insincere gesture of apology or regret from a *commissaire*.

A *commisération* normally accompanies the decision of a *commissaire* to expel a rider for a blatant act of getting a tow, or drafting behind a team car. It traditionally begins with the phrase, 'I'm really sorry, but, as you know, my hands are tied.' And it also traditionally contains the whispered assertion that, 'if it were up to me, I'd turn a blind eye to all of that, anyway. But you know, I don't make the rules. The guys in charge have obviously never raced a bike . . .' etc.

However, it is well known that most *commissaires* are slippery, duplicitous characters and brief journalists and race organisers in the exact opposite terms, describing all riders universally as 'a despicable band of rogues, who would bury their own grandmother for the merest sniff of a chance of grabbing a few bonus seconds at an intermediate sprint. I say throw the rule book at them. Literally.'

Commissaire *nm*

   (i) A judge of matters pertaining to racing bicycles.
  (ii) An armchair fan with a highly judgemental attitude, a Twitter account and no experience of racing bicycles.

Commodité *nf*

The facility with which some riders are able to urinate on the move.

Confiture *nf*

The last moments of pleasure before the pain; like the jam spread on a croissant over breakfast on the morning of a race.

The expression was made famous by Parisian documentary film-maker Hugo Villeneuve whose iconic 1986 work *La Confiture et Le Vinaigre* (*The Jam and the Vinegar*) followed the fortunes of a semi-professional cycling team from the Vosges through an entire racing season. The film was famous for its unflinching treatment of its subjects, whom it documented variously in states of distress, undress, and on the toilet.

In one scene, a rider begs the cameraman to leave him alone as he is trying to apply chamois cream before a race, while another rider is seen pleading on the phone for his wife to come back to him after she discovers that he has been having an affair with a podium girl from Le Havre.

Villeneuve defended this arguably voyeuristic approach by claiming that 'one cannot appreciate one's *confiture* if one has not first drunk one's vinegar'.

No one knew what he meant, although it was still slightly clearer than *Copenhague*.

Contrôleur *nm*

A rider who is repeatedly offering unwarranted advice and dispensing self-regarding wisdom.

Often a *contrôleur* will have a thin, reedy voice, or an unfortunate speech impediment that will render their ministrations still more grating. Some are called Stuart, a name that translates as Benoît in French.

A *contrôleur* never knows when his input is not required. Typically, he might point out to a rider who has tried, and failed, to get in a breakaway, that 'that didn't work out very well, did it?'

Copenhague *nf*

Any race that is devoid of colour or contour is known as a *Copenhague* since, like the Danish capital city, it is grey and flat.

In the Anglophone *peloton*, this is known as a 'pastry', while the Germans refer to it as a 'Berliner', which, coincidentally, also means 'doughnut'.

This entry is one of the most confusing in this book, and should be read more than once.

Corbillard *nm*

Taken from the French word for a hearse, this pejorative term is reserved for the team car into which a rider is reluctantly admitted by the *directeur sportif* at the point of abandoning a race.

The frosty silence that follows a rider's capitulation is often described as living death. As waves of scepticism emanate from the driver's seat, the rider is left feebly protesting his bad fortune/injury/illness to the general incredulity of his employer, who is at that very minute considering whether or not it's worth re-signing this useless wretch for the following season (see *Autopsie*).

The most notorious *corbillard* in the modern *peloton* was, until recently, the terrifyingly bleak Skoda driven by Tinkoff Saxo Bank's terminally serious Bjarne Riis.

The bald, Danish winner of the 1996 Tour de France is famously capable of emitting ultra-high-frequency waves of awkward silence at an inaudible pitch, which cause migrating birds to lose their ability to navigate, and sperm whales to end up inexplicably beached on the west coast of France.

Corde *nf*

The sense of dread and disgust riders have for particularly testing press conferences.

When riders talk of the *corde*, they are referring to a hangman's noose. Not literally, of course, as the last rider to be hanged as a punishment during the Tour de France was the unfortunate Cyrille Menton in 1905. His crime had been to enlist the help of a passing nun to help him dismount his bike after a particularly testing 560-kilometre mountain stage.

In our contemporary, more sanitised age, the *corde* that is dangled in front of riders takes the form of a media grilling during which certain specific, uncomfortable issues will be confronted, such as internal feuding, doping, or riding a bicycle.

The belief is widespread amongst the modern generation of riders that to deal with the press openly and willingly is to place one's head in a noose and allow the feral pack of hacks to tighten it.

This attitude of endemic paranoia is at its most pronounced in the team of the former world champion and relaxed gentleman Mark Cavendish, whose press officer simply throws a length of rope at whichever unfortunate has to take to the stage for the obligatory press conference that day.

'Voilà. C'est à toi la *corde*, aujourd'hui!' (Here you go. You've got the noose today!)

Corniche *nf*

The longed-for status of Monaco residency.

The acquisition of a property close to one of Monte Carlo's famous *corniches* (coastal roads) is a statement to the cycling world that one has made it.

The phrase was first coined by former world champion and Monaco resident Philippe Gilbert, who, on moving to the Principality, declared that from now on his 'eyes would be fixed solely on the glorious, triumphant ascent of the splendour of the *corniche*'.

Not to be confused with *cornichon*.

Cornichon *nm*

The humbling status of Belgian residency.

The acquisition of a property close to one of Belgium's famous *cornichon* (gherkin) pickling plants is a statement to the cycling world that one has failed to make it.

The phrase was first coined by former world champion and Monaco resident Philippe Gilbert, who, on moving back to Belgium, declared that from now on his 'eyes would be fixed solely on the glorious, triumphant consumption of the splendour of the *cornichon*'.

Not to be confused with *corniche*.

Couler *vi*

Fait *couler* les robinets! (Let the taps run!): an overt propensity for crying.

From Raymond Poulidor to Richard Virenque, Greg LeMond and even Mark Cavendish, riders have always blubbed in front of the cameras. However, some riders are believed to have a crying clause in their contracts, carefully negotiated by their agents under the heading 'Image Rights and Sundry Opportunities to Monetise Things'.

In 2014, when Jack Bauer, having spent all day in a two-man breakaway, was denied victory by a matter of a few metres on a dramatic stage into Nîmes, it is widely rumoured that the tears he shed during a post-race interview paid for a new washing machine and a long weekend in a Premier Inn of his choice.

Crêperie *nf*

A low-budget team, in which the limited resources are spread across a wide area until they are paper thin.

It usually folds.

Criailler *vi*

To squawk, to bawl, squall, screech or grouse.

In recent years, the most infamous members of the cycling fraternity to have *criaillé* are the ex-dopers Lance Armstrong, Floyd Landis and Tyler Hamilton. These American riders vehemently protested their innocence, dreaming up ever more elaborate excuses to mask the staggeringly obvious, until the elastic of credibility snapped and the whole thing blew up in their faces.

At that point they started to *criailler,* a process traditionally consisting of a combination of press-conference confessionals, tell-all autobiographies, growing a beard and taking up another pastime such as husky-training or chess, and a tearful interview on *The Oprah Winfrey Show.*

This will be followed, normally, by a poorly attended book-signing in Reading.

Cristallerie *nf*

A *peloton* of such universal nervousness, riddled with fear of falling, that no one wants to race very fast into corners, and the pace slows to something akin to jogging.

However, to maintain the illusion of speed for the television cameras, the riders in a *cristallerie* all drop down to their easiest gear and spin their legs ridiculously fast to mask the fact that they are in fact mincing along at a truly laughable tempo.

Crocodile *nm*

A rider who remains largely motionless until he suddenly erupts in a fury of uncontrolled aggression, provoked by a combination of proximity to human flesh and extreme heat.

No one has earned this epithet more deservedly than the much feared South African sprinter Reggie De Vos, whose sole win came on a stage into Arles on the 1968 Tour de France, during a day that still holds the record for ambient air temperature.

The mercury topped out at 46°C at the white-hot zenith of the afternoon heat. With the race languidly progressing towards the inevitable catch of the breakaway, De Vos, who had been a scarcely visible presence through the first two weeks of racing, suddenly sprinted to the front of the *peloton* and thrashed around wildly in his saddle, his muscular frame twitching madly and his teeth bared with insane intent. The entire *peloton*, shocked at his mania, backed off, terrified, leaving the South African alone on the road. With a shout of 'Ek sal you uit mekaar ruk' (I'll tear you to pieces), De Vos attacked, rode up to the breakaway, repeated his frenzied routine and attacked them too.

He won the race, finishing all alone and still seething with violent intent.

However, word had already reached Arles of his exceptional rage. No one wanted to approach him to tell him he'd won. The podium ceremonials were cancelled that day, and the finish line quickly cleared of spectators.

De Vos is celebrated in his hometown of Mpumalanga with a statue entitled De Krokodil van Nîmes, which, according to local folklore, comes furiously alive on those very rare occasions when the temperature rises above 46°C.

Dressage *nf*

Over-elaborate ankle flexibility leading to a showily
perfect pedal stroke. (See Bradley *Wiggins*.)

D

Dacquois *adj*

Mute, silent, unspeaking.

Literally meaning 'an inhabitant of Dax', it derives from the great, almost entirely forgotten, Jonny Squillante, a resident of the Aquitanian town. He was the son of a well-known aviator and adventurer, Alain Squillante, whose derring-do and extravagant exploits were celebrated widely in the popular press of the inter-war years.

In the belief that only a healthy amount of neglect would toughen his son up, Squillante senior refused to talk to young Jonny, or to allow him to talk, from his fifth to his fifteenth birthday, insisting that 'ten years of mute reflection will make him into the man I have become, and if he is lucky, will achieve some of the wealth and adulation I have earned through the long course of my glorious, continuing, career'.

Young Jonny, taking his father's enforced vow of silence, lived out his ten-year moratorium on talking with complete adherence, withdrawing month by month still further from socialisation. On his fifteenth birthday, he was expecting his father to address him for the first time in a decade, and was greatly looking forward to hearing his own voice in reply.

Yet, when he came downstairs to breakfast, he discovered that his father had left Dax early that morning for Paris, to attend the wedding of a famous casino owner and a film star, and had forgotten entirely about his son's landmark birthday. Without hesitating, the young Squillante silently got together his cycling kit and rode away from home, never to return.

What happened in the intervening years is a matter of conjecture. What is known for sure is that he spent much of his time learning the trade of a professional cyclist. For, in 1937, he signed a contract with Peugeot-Dunlop.

He maintained his voluntary code of silence throughout his solid, if unremarkable, cycling career. He rode seven Tours de France as a mountain domestique, in the service of notable French champions, all of whom were keen to pay tribute to their taciturn teammate.

His lack of language did nothing to diminish his popularity and gave rise to the phrase 'dormir avec le *Dacquois*', a reference to Squillante's status as the perfect roommate. To this day, even though they are scarcely aware of the word's origins, riders still talk of a good night's sleep as 'une nuit *Dacquoise*'.

His 65-year silence was finally broken on his deathbed in 1998, when he was heard to ask for a cup of peppermint tea or, failing that, a Diet Pepsi.

Shortly after that, and before the staff in the nursing home could grant him his wish, he passed silently away.

Dalmatien *nm*

A superannuated climber. A rider whose achievements in the King of the Mountains competition, in which the winner famously wears the polka dot jersey, are so long ago that they might have been filmed in black and white, lending the famous jersey the appearance of a *dalmatien*'s pelt.

Danseur (de corde) *nm*

A tightrope walker, or rider who plots an impossibly narrow-seeming path through a tightly packed *peloton*, never once clipping a pedal or touching elbows.

Such *danseurs* are as fabled within the cycling community as they are respected. They are also the ideal teammate to sit next to at breakfast or on long bus transfers to the start, as they are extremely slender.

But, on the flip side, *danseurs'* feeble upper bodies and general lack of robust build means that they are not very good at linking shoulders, kicking out their legs and jigging up and down drunkenly to 'Come On Eileen' by Dexy's Midnight Runners at the team's Christmas party.

Decrescendo *adv*

Increasing slowness.

To ride *decrescendo* is, for the racing cyclist, like a slow form of death. Taken from the musical term, it is descriptive of a waning or decline of a rider's powers.

The first usage of the term in a cycling context came with the performance of Claude-Achille Debussy's little-performed *Suite pour un Peloton* (see *Orchestration*).

In the '*Alpe*' (see *Alpe*) movement of the suite, a full-scored orchestral theme is reduced, instrument by instrument, until the phrase dwindles to a solo triangle, beaten in plaintive syncopation. Then that, too, stops.

Although this work fell almost into obscurity, it was brought back to the attention of the wider cycling public by classical music aficionado Thomas Voeckler in 2004, who, defending his yellow jersey valiantly through the Pyrenees, declared that 'on the Plateau de Beille I suffered *decrescendo* as if I were Debussy's triangle, alone and tiny in the face of a full orchestra'.

At the time, no one had the faintest idea what Voeckler was talking about, although video footage of the press conference shows most of the journalists nodding sympathetically, as if they totally understood.

Déglutition *nf*

The act of swallowing an energy gel. Not to be confused with *manger* which simply means eating.

This rare medical term for swallowing (for which the verb *avaler* is more commonly used) is preferred by the *peloton*, who are generally disgusted by having to consume these sugary abominations – whose unpalatable gloopiness is matched only by their lurid colour – by the box-load every week.

Since the gels themselves only tangentially relate to actual food as nature intended it to be, so it is deemed appropriate that a word like *déglutition* is used, since it only distantly sounds like a word you might actually use when talking normally.

Degonfleur *nm*

A rider who falls apart with a kilometre to go, like an inflatable arch that suddenly collapses. See *Yates*.

Dentellerie *nf*

Worthless folkloric artisan clutter awarded as a prize on a minor race, sponsored by a local tourism authority. Like a doily.

Although the word *dentellerie* refers specifically to lace-making, it is accepted as meaning any locally produced tat. And since there is scarcely a region of Europe that doesn't claim, in some shape or another, to be the 'home of lace-making', *dentellerie* is universally applicable.

The resale of items of *dentellerie* is an accepted practice, far less risky than the sale of team-issue items through the agency of a *brocante*.

Dépilation *nf*

Normality. A state of entirely normal hairlessness. Nothing unusual.

Désossé *adj*

De-boned, filleted, floppy. Descriptive of the state of tiredness unique to stepping off a bike at the end of a three-week Grand Tour.

Research conducted in 2007 by the School of Osteopaths in Connecticut found that from a sample group of fifty Tour de France riders who underwent examination the day after completing the race, seventeen had forgotten how to walk, nine could no longer hold their heads upright unassisted, three could not use their hands or feet, two had forgotten their names, and one of them had simply crawled into a sleeping bag and locked himself in the airing cupboard.

Destin *nm*

Fate.

Riders are profoundly superstitious. Many believe that their lives are pre-ordained, and that they are merely powerless puppets, whose time on earth is manipulated by unseen powers for unknowable reasons. Certainly, it is widely held that victory, as and when it happens, is written in the stars every bit as much as defeat is unavoidably pre-destined to happen.

The problem with this belief system is that it is all-pervasive, and leads to a degree of world-weary inaction that affects everyday life away from bike races. Family members who do not ride bicycles for a living are normally excluded from this fatalistic belief system and are free to choose their own paths. But the poor riders have no choice in the way their lives pan out. This tension, within the home, can be hard to manage.

A rider's superstition is almost limitless and can be turned to their advantage. For example, it is rare that a rider will lift a finger to help out with the housework at home during their post-season break, since washing-up is not considered part of a rider's *destin*. Neither is DIY, shopping, gardening, hoovering or changing nappies.

Lazing around on the couch watching Eurosport, interestingly, is considered to be *destin*.

Directeur sportif *nm*

A sports director.

A bloke who shouts into a radio and operates the steering wheel of a team car with his knees while simultaneously eating a sandwich and texting his friend in an opponent's team car next to him in the convoy, offering a financial incentive for a team's cooperation on the road.

Usually, a *directeur sportif* is called Gianni and will often wear hastily chosen aftershave bought from the duty-free shop at Charleroi airport on the way back from guiding his team leader to a creditable seventh place in E3 Harelbeke.

Disciple *nm*

A rider who follows every technology fad, like disc brakes and disc wheels.

Discophile *nm*

An admirer of both disc wheels and disc brakes. Often an enthusiastic amateur time-triallist. A bit of a berk.

A rider of less than modest talent who is thrilled by donning ridiculous, teardrop-shaped helmets, figure-hugging skin-suits and climbing aboard bicycles equipped with handlebars that are worth more than the national average monthly wage.

Discrimination *nf*

The unfairly skewed chances of a positive outcome in a race in which there is an awful amount of game-changing technology available for the better-funded teams, like really posh disc wheels.

Given the right kit, even a *discophile* or a *disciple* with limited ability could win a race that has been distorted by *discrimination*.

Doublon *nm*

The use of subterfuge by identical twins. Cycling's most low-rent, but nonetheless uncommon, form of genetic doping.

During the 2014 Tour, which saw the debut of young British rider Simon Yates (see *Yates*), rumours were rife that Adam Yates (see *Yates*), his older brother by one or two minutes, was being smuggled around France in the boot of the Orica GreenEDGE team bus, and that they would take turns to ride, each brother being treated to a rest day every other stage.

These rumours, though furiously denied at the time, gained further traction when Simon Yates (see *Yates*) gave an interview to the *New York Times* in which he claimed to be Sean Yates (see *Yates*), who isn't even his brother Adam Yates (see *Yates*), and is in fact thirty-two years older than him and used to be a gardener in Sussex, as well as wearing the yellow jersey on the 1994 Tour de France.

Druide *nm*

Any rider with a homespun or eccentric recipe or preparation.

The hallmark of a *druide* is his inability to see that the quackery he espouses, and to which he cleaves, is undeniably ineffective and quite possibly illegal.

The more his eccentricities irk his teammates at the dinner table, the more the *druide* is liable to persist. Such figures in the past have included Geoffroy Baladins, and his famous snakeskin ravioli, as well as Chris Froome, the winner of the 2013 Tour de France, during which he subsisted solely on Kenyan water radishes, leading to dramatic weight loss and a progressive change in his accent.

But by far the most infamous *druide* was, without doubt, Anik Bonepart, the extraordinary lank-haired French-Canadian domestique from the American 7-Eleven team, who arrived at the start of the 1995 Tour with a vulture in a cage. For breakfast every morning, he would eat a vulture egg, fried, and often with dippy bread.

Mysteriously, the scavenging bird was stolen from its cage during the night after Stage Eight. His teammate Lance Armstrong (see *Astronaute*) has recently confessed, under subpoena, to his involvement in the avian theft.

'It was looking at me in a funny way, Oprah,' Armstrong tearfully admitted in 2012. 'It was either him, or me.'

Dunkerque *nf*

The inevitable future demise of British cycling dominance on the Continent.

Emmaillotement *nm*

An entanglement of jerseys (*maillots*).

The rare state of grace that great riders attain when, like Peter Sagan did, they simultaneously hold the yellow jersey, the green jersey and the World Champion's rainbow jersey.

Showing off, basically.

E

Eau bénite *nm*

To pass *eau bénite*, or holy water, during an anti-doping urine test is an act of extreme piety.

It is, in a world full of doubt and suspicion, the ultimate expression of a clean conscience, devoid of all the ambiguities contained within the description *blanchâtre*.

The devout Basque climber Argider Arkaitz first coined the phrase in 2003 when requesting that his personal priest bless the flow of urine during his ablutions. After some confusion with the regulations, the World Anti-Doping Agency (WADA) and the UCI ruled that this was indeed possible, and issued him with the world's only Belief Necessitated Cleric Accompaniment Micturition Exemption (BNCAME).

Thus it became a common sight for the tiny rider to be seen walking up the steps of the anti-doping caravan at races, followed by a man in a cassock, swinging an incense burner and chanting Basque hymnals.

While Arkaitz's attitude to passing *eau bénite* was indeed blameless, the same could not be said for his great rival, the Australian firebrand Kevin Ilic, whose pugnacious approach to matters concerning anti-doping led him to a string of notoriously fractious encounters with the authorities, the public, teammates and the media.

Ilic didn't spare religion either. A consistent critic of the Catholic Church, which he considered to have played a significant part in the omertà conspiracy to keep doping habits hidden, he staged a one-man protest during the 2007 Tour de France. During the second rest day of that year's race, he stormed into the Église Saint-Martin in Pau, shouted 'turn this into wine!' and started to urinate into the font, until he was wrestled to the floor by a passing group of South Korean nuns.

Éboueur *nm*

A dustman.

This word harks back to the age when riders routinely shared a hotel room while away at races. An *éboueur* is the least popular sort of roommate; someone who sets their alarm for 5.30 a.m. and clatters around the bathroom, knocking over bins, generally banging into things and singing unselfconsciously (see *Aubade*).

Échalote *nf*

A shallot. Or, in a cycling context, landing upside down next to a shallot.

An *échalote* is the inevitable consequence of trying to hold one's place in a particularly fast-moving *échelon*, which has formed on a long, straight section of road next to an onion (or shallot) field.

Échappée *nf*

   (i) A breakaway.
  (ii) A raw state of chafing to the perineum and inner thighs resulting from a day spent in an *échappée*.

Èche *nm*

Bait.

A rider of little or no consequence, who can be readily sacrificed for the greater good of the team.

The nominated victim must be high enough in the General Classification to pose some sort of threat to the team's opponents, but utterly expendable, as the thankless task that awaits him represents simultaneously the end of his challenge and the moment of his greatest glory, riding like a red giant before reverting to the status of white dwarf, as the *peloton* catches him and spits him out the back. He must attack the *peloton*, and force them to chase.

The word itself is whispered with fear and dread by professional cyclists.

Use of this expression can be traced back to the fearsome *directeur sportif* of the late 1950s Alain Beauregard, who would employ with monotonous regularity the tactic of sending an *èche* up the road for other teams to chase. A big bear of a man, the hirsute Beauregard had won three consecutive editions of the Tour of Camembert in the immediate aftermath of the Second World War. He was known throughout the *peloton* as something of a practical joker, but the kind you never really trusted. Or found funny.

Team briefings were universally feared when Beauregard was taking command. If it was your turn to be the *èche* of the day, dangled out front and eventually doomed to being devoured by a voracious *peloton*, Beauregard would produce a maggot from his top pocket, suspend it wriggling in front of you, and then insist that you eat it.

Riders who refused often found themselves without a contract for the following season, or still worse, having to ride the Tour of Britain (see *Bagatelle*).

Échelon *nm*

A ragged, diagonal formation of the *peloton* caught in crosswinds, at which point in the race everyone is suffering with equal pointlessness.

Échelon is believed, by one or two people I have met, to be derived from the word *échalote* (see *Échalote*). Not many others agree.

Effriter (le biscuit) *vtr*

'Crumbling the biscuit' is an expression used widely among French riders of a certain age, who plied their trade during the halcyon years of the 1980s. Its meaning is uncertain.

The late Laurent Fignon, for example, was often heard to express the opinion that a certain rider was running the risk of 'crumbling his biscuit'. Likewise, Bernard Hinault is very fond of talking about how he never once 'had his biscuit crumbled'. Even Thibaut Pinot, as recently as the 2014 Tour de France, was heard talking of the risk that he might not 'reach Paris with [his] biscuit uncrumbled'.

Its usage is passing on to the next generation, with any original sense now so lost in the passage of time as to render it applicable to almost any race situation.

Église *nf*

The anti-doping caravan. As quiet as a confessional stall in a church, and populated by men in mostly white clothing clutching books of rules, drawn up by other men in mostly white clothing a long time ago, who hold a rider's fate in their hands. Fear of damnation and the darkening presence of evil hang in the air. Not even the presence of a mobile air-conditioning unit can extract from the specially adapted camper van the palpable sense of almighty justice and the unknowable mystery of existence.

It is a reasonably hard place to take a pee.

Égouttoir *nm*

A ghastly, thin torso.

Literally meaning a 'draining rack', an *égouttoir* is commonly understood to refer to the ribcage of a worryingly under-weight rider.

Revealed in all its pale glory by the unzipping of a racing jersey on a sun-baked climb, a well-pronounced *égouttoir* will actually mimic the draining function of a drying rack, by funnelling away the rivulets of sweat in the intercostal chan-nels between the bony ridges of the hideously expanded ribcage, allowing the surface of the professional rider's skin to remain dry to the touch.

In recent times, Chris Froome has boasted the most worry-ingly exaggerated and startling-looking *égouttoir*. The Froome 'rack' enjoys a certain fame in its own right, with an epony-mous Twitter account and Instagram handle.

Élyséen *adj*

Tantalisingly remote. Agonisingly distant. Unbelievably unobtainable.

Derived from the Champs-Élysées, the finishing line of the Tour de France.

The usage of the adjective *Élyséen* has become widespread, and is not restricted to descriptions of distant points on the map. In this sense, and in common with the overuse in the English-speaking cycling world of the adjective 'epic', its value has been somewhat diminished, and things that are seemingly trivial can now be described as being *Élyséen*.

For example, riders are often heard to describe particularly satisfying bowel movements, or successfully logging onto high-bandwidth hotel broadband at the first attempt and without resorting to registering an email address, as *Élyséen*.

Embaumeur *nm*

An embalmer. A very particular type of masseur.

The German *soigneur* (see *Soigneur*) Horst Schiffer certainly lived up to this tag. In fact, his ghoulish legend probably gave rise to the expression.

A taxidermist by trade, he had risen through the ranks to become the favourite animal stuffer of Erich Honecker, the reviled premier of a rapidly failing East German state, and his equally reviled wife, Margot. The ruling couple were fond of hunting at their summer estate in Mecklenburg-Vorpommern.

The Honeckers liked to boast of their exploits with the shotgun to visiting dignitaries over dinner, in a function room hung with trophies. But, if truth be told, their actual prowess did not live up to the high standards they set themselves in their anecdotes. Even though the wild boar, unbeknownst to the First Minister and his lady wife, would be heavily drugged before the hunt, and would merely teeter slowly across the

Honeckers' field of vision, they consistently failed to get away a clean kill. Often, in a terrible fit of rage, the first couple of East German politics would finish the poor beast off at point-blank range, emptying a dozen cartridges into the stricken animal.

After that it was over to Schiffer to repair the damage.

This he did with prodigious ingenuity, stitching the boar back together with great craft until the wounds were rendered invisible once again. After that, he would apply the trademark Schiffer signature to the finished trophy; a sly sneer, achieved by a raising of the boar's upper lip, to reveal his terrible, partly reconstructed, teeth.

It was this menacing, disdainful smirk that so appealed to the Honeckers.

When Erich Honecker was removed from power and the German Democratic Republic ceased to exist, Schiffer spiralled into depression. Having been used to the perks of association with high office, he now found himself unemployed and living on welfare payments in Rostock.

It was only when rising German cycling star and future Tour winner Jan Ullrich bumped into him in a Leipzig nightclub that his fortunes changed. The two men bonded instantly, sharing their passion for the music of Talking Heads. Ullrich came to his rescue.

Schiffer became, for many years, the team masseur for the all-conquering T-Mobile squad, kneading the legs of Tour winners Bjarne Riis and Jan Ullrich, as well as Alexander Vinokourov, Andreas Klöden and latterly a young Mark Cavendish.

He is remembered by every rider he worked with as being, in the words of former T-Mobile rider Roger Hammond, 'gruff, arrogant, truculent, unduly aggressive and completely terrifying'. The eight-time British national cyclo-cross champion goes on to recall how 'there was always a horrifying sneer playing at the corner of his mouth'.

'We called him The Embalmer. It was only later that I discovered that he really was one!'

Encoche *nf*

A notch. This can refer to any amusing or slapstick landmark in a rider's career.

This inglorious rite of passage can take many forms: the first time he slips on the sign-on podium, the first dropped musette in a feed zone or even the first televised wee, mistakenly caught live by a passing moto-camera. Riding and finishing a stage with diarrhoea, misreading a route map and attacking too early for an intermediate sprint, taking a wrong turn and colliding with a dog/journalist, having to push a fat American in a mankini to the side on a climb are all well-rehearsed and oft-repeated *encoches*.

These unfortunate, slightly peripheral occurrences, which may at first seem trivial to the outsider, are in fact vital for fostering a feeling of belonging, and are considered important initiation rites for young riders.

It is, therefore, a badge of honour in the *peloton* to have accrued as many of these dubiously earned notches as possible. The Fasso Bortolo team of the early 2000s took this tradition literally, by handing out ceremonial 'notching sticks' to their neo-pros, along with a branded penknife bearing the sponsor's logo. The sticks would then be placed on the dashboard of the team bus, alongside the trophies and soft toys (yetis or cuddly lions) that the team had accrued from wearing yellow or white jerseys.*

Team Sky (see *Ciel*) have, almost inevitably, created an app for their team-issue iPhones, on which their young riders are encouraged to whittle virtual notches on their interactive CGI sticks. The data is then uploaded, or shared instantaneously via Bluetooth, with the coaching staff, where Rod Ellingworth, Head of Morale and Winningness, analyses and ultimately verifies them. If they are deemed to be authentic landmarks, the rider will receive a smiley face emoticon and a bonus of €500,000.

Endimanché *adj*

Dressed up in one's Sunday best, or de-mob happy. Beginning to clock-off.

---

* In the case of Fasso Bortolo, such a display of cuddly toys was extremely rare. In fact, it never happened, since they never won anything, really.

Since the Tour de France traditionally ends on a Sunday (*dimanche*), this term refers to any rider, who, during the final week of the race, starts mentally to shut down, and coast through the closing stages, as if it were the final few days of the school term when teachers can't be arsed any more and you get to watch films and play KerPlunk.

This slackening of concentration is often seen as a sign of weakness to be exploited by one's more alert rivals who are stuck on other, more workman-like days of the week (and can be described as being still *enmardi, enmercredi* or *enjeudi*).

Typical symptoms of a rider being *endimanché* include skipping breakfast, reading the paper very slowly in the mornings on the team bus, stopping at the side of the road to pass the time of day with elderly people and children, and dropping in on any sites of historical interest the route of the Tour might happen to be passing.

Escargot *nm*

A snail. A pejorative term for an unprepossessing cycling fan.

Riders, in fact, have endless reserves of contempt for most cycling fans, although their public utterances will invariably present a very different picture, one in which they praise 'the great passion of the crowd' and express gratitude for the 'huge encouragement' they glean from the 'wonderful supporters'.

Privately, they express very different sentiments.

Traditionally, *escargot* is a description reserved for obsessive, overweight, unsavoury, perspiring, middle-aged French men in string vests and nylon running shorts, who stand outside their camper van (the snail's shell) hollering encouragement at their favourite rider (often Richard Virenque) and abuse at anyone else (normally anyone un-French).

Estivage *nm*

The summering of cycling fans (see *Escargot*), like alpine cattle, on high mountain passes.

Être *vi*

To be.

In the middle of a race, riders often describe reaching a level of existence that pertains only to professional cyclists, in which their memory, emotional life and intellect are subsumed entirely by the relentless demands of otherwise ordinary bodily processes required simply to stay alive, like a beating heart and diaphragm that expands in order to draw oxygenated air into the lungs and thereby begin the cyclical procedure of metabolism.

This is known as *être*.

If a cyclist has reached this unique state of being, his peers will nod in acknowledgement, nudge each other, and point enviously to the rider in question, commentating, 'Regarde Julien. Il *est*.'

Euthanasie *nf*

Riding the Tour of Romandie in Switzerland, with its relaxed approach to suicide.

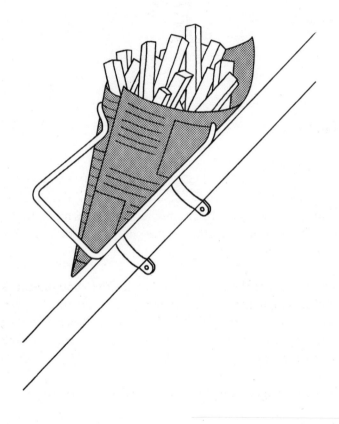

Friterie *nf*

Belgium.

F

Facteur *nm*

The postman.

Traditionally, this is a 'very important' member of the cycling team's staff who goes from hotel room to hotel room, sometimes in the dead of night, or extremely early in the morning, making 'deliveries'.

These days, if the recipient is not in, the consignment is seldom simply left with a neighbour, but is routinely taken back to the sorting office in the hotel foyer, where it can be collected after twenty-four hours upon presentation of valid photographic ID.

If it is not collected within three months it is disposed of.

Factotum *nm*

An odd-job man.

A rider who is not much use really, since they are no good at doing anything in particular, but simply reasonable about doing a bunch of rather unremarkable things, like riding quite hard in valley roads, not falling over on bends, finishing in the top thirty on rare occasions and only when it scarcely matters, and standing in the second row back during the annual team photograph.

A *factotum* is highly unlikely to *faire* (see *Faire*).

Faire *vtr*

To do.

In cycling, this means to contribute to the race in some form or another, rather than finish every single time, anonymously, in the middle of the bunch, having achieved nothing. *Faire* means actually doing stuff, making your mark, getting yourself noticed. Often it will involve *être*.

It is considered one of the highest accolades if one's peer recognises that, from time to time, one has been seen to *faire*.

Faisan *nm*

A pheasant.

An overly well-groomed, strutting, dim-witted rider, given to great shows of pride, but ultimately exceptionally easy to shoot down.

Few riders in the history of the Tour have fulfilled this stereotype more completely than the legendary Benito Benvenuti, a foppish all-rounder of the mid 1970s. Benvenuti, riding for the short-lived and hugely under-achieving Cornetto Team (sponsored by Wall's Ice Cream), was forever changing his appearance in order to generate headlines.

Dubbed 'The Bowie of the Bike', Benvenuti would style himself differently for every Tour he started. Sometimes he would bring a space gun to the start ramp of the opening time trial and shoot imaginary laser beams into the crowd. On other occasions, he would have extra details sewn into the fabric of his racing jersey, like a smoking gun in a holster, an exploding mushroom cloud or a shark's fin.

Most infamously, for the final stage of the 1978 Tour, he arrived on the Champs-Élysées in a deerstalker and tartan cape, puffing away on a pipe. His homage to Sherlock Holmes led to a record UCI fine of 100,000 Swiss Francs being levied. Benvenuti protested wildly, but continued his headlong, publicity-hungry charge.

He arrived at Fleurance for the opening time trial of the 1979 Tour dressed from head to toe as an Egyptian mummy. Only on the start ramp did he discard his bandages, peeling them off to reveal the fact that he was wearing nothing whatsoever underneath. He was arrested on the spot and publicly escorted in handcuffs along the route of the prologue and into a waiting car at the finish line, trailing his costume bandages as he went and blowing kisses to the crowd.

He was later charged with contravention of, and convicted under the terms of, the rarely used French by-law of 'disrespecting a race of bicyclists by dint of clothing'.

Fauconnier *nm*

A falconer.

A virtuoso *directeur sportif* who appears to have his charges entirely at his command, answering to his call and returning to their master.

It is thought that the celebrated sports director Félix Bergerac of the late 1940s first gave rise to the expression when he took to wearing a leather protective cuff on his right arm, and dressing his riders in studded collars with light plumage attached to their racing caps.

In more recent times, English football manager Sam Allardyce has credited Bergerac with influencing his thinking. During his reasonably successful spell in charge of Bolton Wanderers, Allardyce routinely tossed scraps of raw meat through the air at his players at half time.

Fausset *nm*

Falsetto. The overly high-pitched voice with which one tries to bluff out and mask one's distress.

For example, in answer to the question, 'How are the legs?' when riding up a particularly gruelling and steep climb, one might answer, in a revealing and laughable *fausset*, 'Fine, actually. Really good.'

Féodalisme *nm*

The dark and complex hierarchy of interconnected relationships within the convoy of team cars at the back of the race.

The seemingly high-tech world of liveried vehicles with bicycles on the roofs in fact closely resembles a complete and holistic medieval world. Bartering, for example, is commonplace, as bottles, food, kit and phone chargers are swapped and traded liberally between opposing teams. Riders, the foot soldiers of this organised society, are often bought and sold like cattle at market, with the transactions being rubber-stamped by the simple shake of a hand through the open window of a Skoda estate car.

But, more significantly, a pecking order is established along feudal lines between the various *directeurs sportifs* at the wheels of the team cars.

Sometimes the power is wielded by certain individuals who might have some awful hold over a peer, relating to their own less-than-trustworthy riding careers. There's nothing like a doping scandal to wreck a career.

Although actual examples of blackmail are rare, it is quite commonplace for 'armies' to be 'raised', and whole teams will mysteriously be seen to be riding for opposing teams, without any clear purpose. This is often viewed as evidence of *féodalisme*, and is almost certainly the result of a feudal lord calling in a favour or two.

Fétu *nm*

A wisp of straw.

'Avoir les jambes de *fétu*' describes a moment of prodigious feebleness when the legs feel, literally, like wisps of straw.

This phenomenon, although it can strike at any given moment during a race, is often best observed in riders trying to cope with the demands of life off their bikes. In meeting the basic requirements of a functioning existence away from their sport, most professional cyclists usually pull up woefully short. In fact, they are so attuned to the one-dimensional demands of pedalling that anything requiring more variety or a different kind of strain is often quite beyond them.

Activities that cause their overworked legs to buckle and wilt like wisps of straw include the popular pastimes of standing and walking, both of which feature extensively in the everyday habits of the non-cycling population. Running is something no cyclist has ever done.

It was to avoid the dreaded feeling of *fétu* that Maurice Garin, the winner of the inaugural Tour de France in 1903, demanded to be taken everywhere by a gilt-encrusted sedan chair, transported to his hotel by hundreds of willing admirers wherever he went. Moreover, and not uncontroversially, he insisted that his helpers were all women aged under twenty-five.

Garin famously declared that since he'd 'crucified himself for the love of France', it was not unreasonable for him to believe that 'the good daughters of France might mop [his] brow in return, and wash away the trials of the day in the salt tears of their sisters'.

Garin's extrovert use of the sedan chair to save his legs was an act of self-aggrandising pomposity briefly reintroduced by the infamous Lance Armstrong (see *Astronaute*) a century later, on the 2003 Tour.

Armstrong became accustomed to being lifted from his bike at the end of every stage, and carried aloft to his team bus on a carbon fibre US Postal-liveried platform, modelled to look like an X-Wing Starfighter from *Star Wars*, and supported by a quartet of shaven-headed Belgian ex-marines, whom he affectionately referred to as his 'Oompa-van-der-Loompas'.

Fierté *nf*

Pride.

Above all, to succeed at the highest level, a rider must exhibit the requisite *fierté*.

It was a common belief, up until the advent of sports psychologists with their fancy talk of motivation and chimps, that whatever else might hamper him, the rider must be pumped full of self-respect, to an uncomfortably pressurised level.

However talented a bike rider might prove himself to be as a junior, however many victories he might have achieved on his way to becoming a professional, it was commonly, almost unquestioningly, accepted that he would not amount to much 's'il manque la *fierté* nécessaire', if he lacked the necessary pride.

Thus it came to be considered both routine and important that riders were schooled to an extraordinary degree in the science of High Self Regard. Birthdays, for example, if they happened during the Tour, would be celebrated, not by a cake and a sing-song, but with a long and detailed speech made by the rider celebrating the anniversary, recounting the many ways in which he excelled, and would continue to excel.

As a result of such self-conscious preening, the *peloton* was not a place for the meek. The mild-mannered 1954 Tour de France favourite Yves Goddard withdrew from the race on the morning of the Grand Départ and was never seen again at a bike race, after suffering from a complete collapse in his pride. He had, in own words, 'woken up that morning feeling as if there may be other people in the race who were at least my peers, if not my superiors'.

Over breakfast he confided in his *directeur sportif* Jacques Reblochon, who advised him in no uncertain terms that 'the Tour could be won by riders overcoming illness, treachery, misfortune and disaster, but never by a rider with low to middling self-esteem'. Goddard packed his bags and left.

Le Monde newspaper roundly lambasted him the following day in a scathing front-page editorial denouncing him as a bust flush, someone with 'une *fierté* crevée', or punctured pride.

This led, briefly, to Goddard becoming the face of Rustines Vulcanisation puncture repair kits, in an innovative marketing campaign which was mimicked some forty years later by Pizza Hut's use of failed England football penalty takers.

Fondue *nf*

The dynamics of a breakaway group, in which everyone is sharing the work equally, but which is ultimately doomed. The point of comparison with the culinary concept of a cheese or oil fondue is that everybody takes it in turns, but in the end they all get cooked.

Forçage *nm*

Dutiful aggression.

Derived from the agricultural term for forcing growth, *forçage* describes an artificial, premeditated, contrived, but nonetheless counterintuitive, attack in conditions that are not conducive to such behaviour, such as a bitterly cold northern European early-season race. In many ways it is the opposite of its sunnier, more Mediterranean cousin *panache*.

Riders who demonstrate the capacity for *forçage* are the subject of universal admiration from pundits, journalists and commentators alike, and are credited with enlivening other-wise processional editions of gloomy-looking events, such as the now extinct Fifteen and a Half Days of Le Havre.

Fratricide *nm*

The ultimate cycling taboo. Contributing nothing to a break-away, and then outsprinting one's 'brothers' to take the win.

Not to be confused with the genuine and tragic case of fratricide that ended with the disembowelling of time-triallist Piotr Lulanskh during the 2006 Tour de France, a crime for which his brother, and former Cofidis rider Oleg Lulanskh, is still imprisoned in Nantes. He is due to be released on parole in 2024.

Francophobe *adj*

Unfair.

Any race route described as *francophobe* is deemed to be gro-tesquely unfair; packed with climbs that are unreasonably climby, descents that are a bit too downhill, winds that are too windy and sprints that are too sprinty.

Froomage *nf*

A testing predicament which requires extreme measures. Like being stranded halfway up Mont Ventoux without a bike. In a bike race.

Frottement *nm*

The elbow-rubbing proximity of riders in an unpleasantly closely-packed *peloton*, passing through a suddenly narrowed section of road (see *Caque*).

Fumoir *nm*

A smokehouse.

The acrid, choking bar in some nondescript northern French town in which existential decisions about riders' futures are made by overweight middle-aged ex-pros with a terminal smoking habit who now find themselves, surprisingly, in charge of a cycling team. When the final decision to release a rider from the team is reached, the door opens, and a whiff of white cigarette smoke is emitted, Vatican-style.

Everyone in cycling knows that a puff of white smoke is bad news.

Galion *nm*

An overly large team bus (see *Ciel*).

G

G *nm*

A rider from Wales.

Gâcheur *nm*

A botcher. A slovenly wretch.

Anyone who does not meet the ridiculously exacting standards of the professional cyclist and whose standards fall,
however minutely, short of complete excellence, will be
known as a *gâcheur* – a corner-cutter, a good-for-nothing
make-do-and-mender and a cad. Not to be confused with a
bouif, whose ingenuity demands respect. There is nothing to
celebrate in the *gâcheur*.

Nothing offends the uniquely precious sensibility of the
roadie more than a set of almost invisibly scuffed cranks or a
tiny nick in the handlebar tape. The merest hint that one
might perch atop a saddle set, however imperceptibly,
crooked would be enough to send any respectable member of

the *peloton* reeling across the hotel foyer, reaching for the toilet doors and succumbing to an understandably vigorous bout of nausea (see *Ajustage*).

Routinely, the slovenly and despised *gâcheurs* find themselves ostracised. Their detractors will multiply as their allies and supporters melt away, until they descend into an isolated private hell from which it is almost impossible to return. They breakfast alone, they ride alone at the back of the bunch, and they aren't followed by any of their teammates on Twitter or Instagram.

At one point in cycling's history though, there was an interesting move away from fanatically applied standards, and towards casual sloppiness. In the late 1990s, a little-remembered Dutch team of *gâcheurs* bore the name of their sole patron, Zeppelin Girls, an infamous Amsterdam nightspot.

Unable to get a bike sponsor, nor sign up a kit sponsor, the riders would all turn up at races looking as if they had never met one another, which they probably hadn't. They rode numerous different brands of bike, and wore homespun kits, each bearing little relation to their teammates', onto which they had, with various degrees of success, managed to velcro the Zeppelin Girls logo.

Such unconformity became their unique selling point.

Drawn from a pool of what the team management considered to be harshly rejected, unfairly misunderstood talent, the Zeppelin riders prided themselves on their rough appearance and would often flaunt rust patches on their chains and food stains on their bib-shorts. Their *soigneurs* propped up the bar in the hotel from lunchtime onwards, and would never bother massaging their riders. And the mechanics ended up working part time as roadies for nearby rock concerts instead of mending and preparing their riders' bikes.

They were, for a while, furiously popular with the crowd, who appreciated their maverick appearance. But inevitably the cycling authorities took a dim view and they were denied a wild-card entry to the 2000 Tour de France, despite their team owner and former brothel magnate Willy Snelling offering the organisers a very public, very substantial bribe.

The team went into liquidation one month before that year's Tour. The short-lived *gâcheur's* Zeppelin Girls jerseys, however, are highly prized and collectable, and often command lively bidding wars on eBay, much like the Hornby cycling sets described under *ambulatoire*, whose entry concluded with a similar paragraph.

Gaffe *nf*

Celebrating a victory too early, and being beaten on the line as a consequence (see *Imbroglio* and *Encoche*).

Galanterie *nf*

Fair play. Sporting behaviour. A pejorative term.

The professional *peloton* is, by nature, dismissive of riders who exhibit excessive *galanterie*. The cycling equivalent of laying one's cape over a puddle for a lady to step over may look good to the outside world, but it is simply considered a sign of weakness within the ranks.

In fact, a genuine act of selflessness, such as giving a team-mate your wheel when he punctures his own is interpreted as effectively raising a white flag of surrender.

Far better to ride past as if you hadn't noticed.

Galbé *adj*

Sensuously curvaceous. To describe a climb as *galbé* would indeed be a compliment.

Traditionally *galbé* is a term reserved for cocktail-lounge appreciation of women with hour-glass figures by lascivious bon viveurs sporting waxed moustaches and tuxedos.

It was adopted into cycling parlance by the legendary 'Playboy des Alpes' Félix Chamonix during the 1952 Tour de France. Chamonix asserted, after a particularly gruelling mountain stage that resulted in over a third of the field abandoning, that the two climbs of the Col du Télégraphe and the Col du Galibier, when ridden back to back, were 'things of treacherous beauty, *galbés* like the thighs, back and derrière of a siren of the silver screen'.

The description stuck with the cycling public.

In fact a decade later, Jacques Brel, the Belgian chanteur and Tour de France enthusiast, gave it greater popularity still when he incorporated the term into his popular love song, 'Chloé'. Chloé, the subject of his young hero's adoration, was a hefty farm girl from Lille with a heart of gold and whom the charismatic singer described, in a particularly ecstatic stanza, as being '*galbée* comme le Galibier', a typically Brel-esque play on words.

Galéjer *vi*

To lie.

Lance Armstrong (see *Astronaute*) is the undisputed leader in this field. But he is not the first celebrated fibber.

It was probably Simon Vechter, known to many as The German, because of his Teutonic heritage, who was the first rider to be feted for his ability to *galéjer*. The tiny Alsatian climber claimed to have won Liège–Bastogne–Liège in 1942, a year in which it was not raced.

Away from cycling, in 1948 Vechter gained notoriety throughout Western Europe when, a full four years before Sir Edmund Hillary's assault on Everest, he claimed to have become the first man on top of the tallest mountain on earth.

Indeed several newspapers, including *Le Monde*, *The Times* and *El País*, published the same grainy photograph of Vechter planting the flag of his home region of Alsace-Lorraine on top of the Himalayan peak, clad in nothing more than his thick winter Team Peugeot cycling jersey and shorts. His fraudulence was only unmasked when a sharp-eyed picture editor, poring over the image with a magnifying glass, was able to discern the clear silhouette of a tractor, pulling a trailer full of manure, in the background.

The mystery remained as to why Simon Vechter chose to lie with such abandon, and with such a self-destructive outcome, as he was a very accomplished rider in his own right. His three stage wins at the Tour de France were testimony to the fact that he undeniably possessed great talent. So, the wilful dismantling of his own reputation has puzzled historians of the sport ever since.

The Tasmanian psychiatrist Naomi Wolfenwitz would later cite the career of Vechter in her doctoral thesis 'The Unbearable Lightness of Brilliance: A clinical case study of mendacity and genius' (1993) in support of her assertion that an individual's understanding of their own great potential can provoke a psychosis born from fear of failure that tends towards self-annihilation. She identifies this as Vechter Syndrome.

The modern *peloton* also bears witness to the unusual career of Simon Vechter in its geographically inaccurate adoption of the term 'galéjer comme l'Allemand' (to lie like the German). Vechter was, of course, French.

The last recorded use of that phrase was by the seven-time green jersey wearer Erik Zabel, who, when finally admitting to his doping past, addressed the French public on national television with an apology for having spent the best part of the previous decade, in his words, 'galéjant comme l'Allemand'.

It was also the first time that Zabel admitted to being German, having previously claimed to have been born on a comet and fallen to earth swaddled in 'bubble wrap from space'.

Garçon *nm*

A mildly untrustworthy domestique, who is storing up a burgeoning sense of injustice, and will one day demand pay-back, like a waiter dropping the bill onto a restaurant table (see also *Bailli*).

Claude Beaupoint was one such *garçon*. For twelve Tours he loyally rode as a support rider for the underperforming Canadian team McCluskey's Salmon, serving a hopelessly ill-equipped team leader Chris McCluskey, who never once made the GC top 20 in a decade of trying.

Day after day, Beaupoint would uncomplainingly drop back to the convoy, pick up McCluskey's water and favourite salmon-paste sandwiches, and ferry them back up to the front of the race, only for the leader to fall out of serious contention at the earliest possible moment when the real racing began.

Beaupoint, though remaining stoically loyal, was saving up his resentments.

On Stage Twenty-One of the 1992 Tour, his final race, Beaupoint rode alongside McCluskey just before the race reached Paris and presented him with a long, handwritten invoice for services rendered, including a demand for compensation totalling $1m that 'should not, under any circumstances, be paid in the form of tinned salmon'.

Gaucherie *nf*

Racing in the United Kingdom, Australia, or any other country that insists on driving on the wrong side of the road.

Gaulois *nm*

An old-school French *directeur sportif* who drinks pastis and is shamelessly addicted to cigarettes.

Géologue *nmf*

A rider with local knowledge of a specific mountain range.

There are many *géologues* in the contemporary *peloton* with a deep understanding of the colossal splendour of the Alps, as well as a large number of climbers with an excellent knowledge of the breathtaking Dolomites mountain range that divides Austria and Trentino in northern Italy, and which formed the backdrop to a stupendously bloody front line in the First World War, the setting for Ernest Hemingway's masterpiece *A Farewell to Arms*.

But, interestingly, there are far fewer with a working understanding of the tectonic pressures that created the Kent Downs and how the chalk seams determine the gradients of the climbs around Westerham, and where the local bus routes cross the boundary between Kent and the London Borough of Bromley. And where to get a half-decent sandwich in Tonbridge.

Giration *nf*

An unsettled, irresolute and unpredictable state of mind during a bike race such as the Tour de Romandie (see *Euthanasie*), brought about by the imminent and worrying prospect of having to ride the Giro d'Italia, a race of such sadism that few riders survive more than a few editions before suffering permanently from dreams of bears emerging from Apennine forests to tear them limb from limb.

Gong *nm*

An Olympic medal. Pejorative.

Specifically applicable to a medal that is won by a half-decent rider who just happened to get a bit lucky on the day, simply because they got in the breakaway and didn't puncture. Or, if winning a *gong* on the track, they benefited from £3m of lottery funding just to develop their socks in a wind tunnel.

Graillon *nm*

A scrap of burnt fat.

The state an underprepared and overweight Northern Hemisphere rider finds himself in after the first day competing in an early-season race in the glaring heat of the Southern Hemisphere summer.

Gramophone *nm*

A rider who talks incessantly about weight.

Grippe-sou *nm*

A tight-wad, or penny-pincher. Not uncommon in the professional *peloton*.

Any rider who is unreasonably motivated by money is liable to earn this label, but when this obsessive maximising of one's earnings is coupled with a total unwillingness to buy a round of drinks, then the nickname *grippe-sou* (literally, 'stuck-penny') will surely, deservedly, follow.

Italy's largely anonymous sprinter Fabio Conti, who rode in a support role for the now defunct German team Gerolsteiner in the early 2000s, was a notorious *grippe-sou*.

A rider who would regularly feature in the day's breakaway simply to earn a few quid, Conti would commit to memory the entire prize pot for every race on the calendar, including intermediate sprint primes as well as the approximate cash value of any silverware/glassware or local salami (see *Dentellerie*) that was presented to the rider during the podium ceremonials.

It is rumoured that in retirement he has opened a small museum in the garage at his parents' home in Umbria where one can view all the items he was ever gifted by sponsors, displayed in order of value. The most prized exhibit is an Alpaca poncho from the Tour of Peru in 2005. The €20 entrance fee to the museum includes free use of the Conti family toilet, and 10% off your next visit.

Conti also made unwelcome headlines in 2008 for charging his small but loyal fan base €5 for his autograph, €10 for an awkward photo outside a team bus and €20 for a short conversation about his chances in the bunch sprint (€30 if you wished to upgrade to the 'executive conversation' that involved him actually answering).

€50 would buy you dinner for three (including Conti's mother) at a restaurant of Conti's mother's choice (meal not included), while a cool €2,000 would see you jetting off to Florida with the Italian and his girlfriend Valeria (flights and accommodation not included).

Groupuscule *nm*

An ignoble and reviled group of stragglers. Not to be confused with the more common term 'grupetto', which is invariably a courageous, altruistic and valiant group. Membership of the *groupuscule* is the opposite of a badge of honour. It has been said that it is cycling's equivalent of the estate agency profession.

There comes a time in any bike race, mostly unseen by the television cameras, when there is the inevitable formation at the back of the convoy of a tiny group of hopeless cases, feebly crawling towards the finishing line, variously doing battle with dysentery, halitosis, gum disease, scabies or other debilitating disorders – or simply a colossal lack of ability. Their physical ghastliness is mirrored only by their moral torpor.

So craven and dishonest is the *groupuscule* that it will stop at nothing to achieve its goal of avoiding elimination: stealing food from roadside picnickers, cutting corners when the road goes round a hairpin, holding onto the backs of cars with liberal, desperate abandon and running into local pharmacies screaming at the staff behind the counter that they should hand over any 'purple or dangerous-looking pills'.

Guillotine *nf*

The top step of the podium when one shouldn't be there.

This applies to a race that was supposed to have been won by someone from the local area. Someone more important. Someone who had paid good money to ensure that he would win.

The sense of unease these unfortunate winning riders feel as they fumble with their champagne corks and nervously mismanage the customary kissing of the podium girls, in the knowledge that no one, neither the crowd, nor the organisation, wanted them to win, is only heightened by the traditional appearance of knitting needles among the lookers-on. The podium ceremony is conducted in total silence, save for the clickety-clack sound of jumpers being knitted, and the accompanying murmur of 'purl one, knit one . . .'

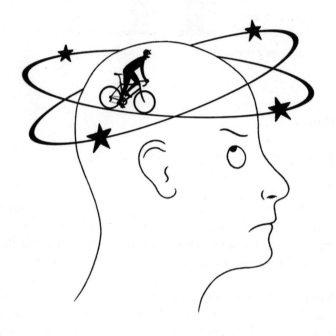

Hérode *nm*

A grizzly, senior rider who takes great delight in the (occasionally fatal) suffering of newly qualified professionals.

H

Haire *nf*

Terrible suffering. Literally, a 'hair shirt'.

As if riding the Tour de France were not hard enough when fully fit, most riders are, at any given time, suffering from some affliction or impairment that is steadily aggravated to the point of maddening discomfort by the long hours in the saddle. This state of affairs is known as *porter une haire*.

Riders of the inter-war era suffered the most. Huge privations were a way of life. It was not uncommon for riders to escape death by a whisker in pursuit of glory on the Tour. They were often found unconscious by the side of the road, after passing out from the effects of open wounds to the buttocks, partially burned hands (caught up in the furnaces from frame-makers' forges when trying to adhere to the Tour's repressive regulations concerning self-sufficient repairs) or the debilitating ravages of the final stages of Spanish flu, or even, in the tragic case of London cyclist Ronny Heslop, the bubonic plague.

Heslop succumbed to the plague during the 1923 Tour, passing away during the night after completing the 680 kilometres from Grenoble to Compiègne. His body was left at the Hôtel de la Poste near the finish line, where a sprig of thyme was mysteriously inserted up his nose and a bible placed at his side. He was later interred in a pauper's grave.

Such extraordinary hardiness endures through the ages, even to this day, where riders uphold the tradition of simple stoicism that goes with the territory of being a bike racer.

In more recent times, Darren Drawbridge, the Australian neo-pro from Orica GreenEDGE, forgot to snip off the sticky-out label from the inside of his brand-new team jersey, and rode the entire 2013 Tour de France with a slight itch just under his ribs on his right-hand side.

At times Drawbridge became so distracted by this persistent tickle that he even pulled alongside his team leader Simon Gerrans and asked him for advice.

'Fucking pull yourself together,' came the reply from the Melbourne-educated former Milan–San Remo winner. 'You fucking Sheila,' he added, before sending the unfortunate Drawbridge back to fetch lots and lots of bottles from the team car, which, when delivered to him by the chastened young rider, Gerrans quite deliberately emptied out onto the road, muttering, ' . . . itchy fucking jumper'.

And then adding, 'for fuck's sake'.

Hanséatique *adj*

Hanseatic.

There is a widely held suspicion within the Mediterranean cycling world (Spain, France and Italy) that their historical pre-eminence is being consistently eroded by a loose affiliation of rival, yet cooperating teams whose headquarters are all near, or at least close to, the North Sea and Baltic coasts. This, it is believed, is a part of the continuing power struggle at the heart of world cycling.

This is known as the *hanséatique* theory, in acknowledgement of the four hundred years of the Hanseatic League of merchant states.

While most observers dismiss this notion as paranoid nonsense, in 2015 the Spanish newspaper *El País* captured covert footage of a secret Masonic-looking meeting at the Bremen headquarters of German pro-continental team Schelling Spedition und Logistik, attended by a core group of important figures from the cycling offshoots of the United Kingdom, the Netherlands, Poland and Denmark.

Sir Dave Brailsford (see *Ciel*) was one of a number of team managers present. He was filmed, dressed in Hanseatic medieval garters and breeches, talking fluent Low German to a group of tyre manufacturers from Groningen about a free-trade agreement which would see inner tubes arriving by clipper along the Thames, and thither being transported post-haste towards Mancunia.

Godspeed.

Harem *nm*

The sycophantic, emasculated circle of riders from a variety of teams, who will nonetheless find themselves working hard for the *sultan* of the race, under whose spell they have fallen (see *Astronaute*).

Harengère *nf* (pej)

A fishwife. Or, put more simply, a rider whose odour is off-putting.

The Danish *rouleur* of the mid 1990s, Rasmus Frederiksen, never washed in his entire career. But he also never crashed in his entire career.

This was largely attributed to the fact that the bunch kept a protective distance from him at all times, so that effectively he was riding in a bubble within the *peloton*, ensuring that he always had time to react to a fall ahead of him.

It was said by his former teammate Brian Holm that Frederiksen smelt 'like his body parts had been dismembered and left out on the patio, or maybe decking, in the sun. To rot. And then put back on his body. Rotting. Or something. A bit like that anyway. I don't know what happened to him, actually. Last I heard he'd moved to Poland with a lady he'd met in a petrol station when he was driving home for Christmas in Aarhus.'

Hibou *nm*

An owl.

A pejorative term for the kind of unsmiling, earnest, oddly unsettling cycling fan that gathers outside a team bus at the start of a race.

An *hibou* is capable of total watchful immobility for hours on end, and occasionally demonstrates a rare ability for turning their head through 180 degrees at the slightest sense that a rider might be disembarking from another team bus directly behind them.

Hiéroglyphe *nm*

The handwritten, and therefore largely illegible, tactical instructions and race profile details, diligently prepared by the team's *directeur sportif* and taped to the stem of a bike before a race.

Hospice *nm*

A berth on the roster of a lesser team, which a once great rider joins to eke out the fading embers of a career and collect one or two years of significantly reduced salary (see *Lotto*).

Hospitalité *nf*

Unjustifiable savagery, sadism and wilful persecution, meted out by wealthy fans of the Tour de France.

It is often the experience of riders that the vilest abuse comes from the cordoned-off hospitality marquees which predominate in every little town and village on the route of the Tour de France.

A combination of free alcohol and an inflated sense of self-worth that results from the wearing of an accreditation bracelet, giving you access to the exclusive roadside berth, leads normally mild-mannered locals to shower riders with a litany of foul expletives as they pass by the hospitality tent.

As a result, you will often hear *directeurs sportifs* warning their charges over the radio of the presence of an *hospitalité* around the corner, as if it were a dangerous bend or a treacherous road surface. Some riders have such an inbuilt fear of hospitality tents that they will veer over to the far side of the ride to avoid the possibility of having stinging champagne thrown into their eyes or a prawn velouté splattered through their spokes.

The final stage of the Tour de France on the Champs-Élysées circuit is particularly traumatic for those with an irrational fear of *hospitalité*, since corporate entertainment areas dominate both sides of the avenue between the Place de la Concorde and the finish line. It is customary for a cluster of riders to avoid this section of the race altogether, until the very last of the eight laps of the Champs-Élysées.

They manage to cut these laps out by hiding in the darkness in the tunnel at the back of the circuit where the television cameras go black, as no TV signal is possible. Although this is a technical infringement of the race rules and should result in their ejection from the Tour, the *commissaires* tend to turn a blind eye, and consider the drunken middle-management types guzzling sparkling wine and canapés with the same total disdain that the riders do.

It is generally understood, therefore, within the *peloton*, that when a rider publicly praises the wonderful *hospitalité* of the French population and thanks them for 'their marvellous support, which makes the great race the spectacle it is', he means the exact opposite.

Hotte *nf*

A bag. Literally, a sack, as in 'la *hotte* du Père Noël', or 'Santa's sack'.

An *hotte* is a hold-all containing the various superstitious, sentimental or simply strange items a rider brings with him in his luggage on a three-week stage race.

In the case of British Tour de France yellow jersey wearer Chris Boardman, this often meant the inclusion of a full Airfix kit, complete with wooden assembly board, the correct Humbrol emulsions (matt black, olive drab, desert yellow etc.), a scalpel with sufficient replacement blades and a CD of *ELO's Greatest Hits*.

His roommates often complained that, though the Wirral-based prologue specialist generally kept himself to himself and exhibited fastidious tidiness, their sleep would be disturbed at regular intervals as Boardman replayed 'Sweet Talkin' Woman' on an endless loop and shaved away at moulded fuselage edges to acquire a perfectly smooth, yet sufficiently scarified surface on which the solvent might best bond.

Other riders have taken a less practical approach to their 'must-have' items for a three-week road trip around France. The content of each man's *hotte* is as revealing as it is occasionally puzzling.

No one knew, for example, why George Hincapie carried his grandmother's wedding dress around, nor how he kept it so perfectly pressed.

Humanisme *nm*

The sporting philosophy, or school of thought, that led certain directors of the Tour de France in the post-war years to shorten the average stage distance from 500 to 200 kilometres, and, in 1919, ban the widespread and unregulated use of the blunderbuss by the race *commissaires*.

Hyène *nf*

Hyenas are not uncommon in the professional *peloton*. But, unlike their namesakes in the natural world, their cycling cousins, generally speaking, do not hunt in packs.

But they do slink around for hours, friendless and unlovely, waiting to tear the flesh from the exhausted cadavers of more honourable beasts than them.

The *hyène* is the one rider at the back of the group of break-away riders who has not done a stroke of work. He is also the one rider, who, because he has not done a stroke of work, will win the stage.

He will normally celebrate by pointing to a bicep, or miming the cradling of a new-born infant as if to proclaim how blessed he is by God. He is not well-liked.

He is normally, but not exclusively, Italian.

Infrarouge *adj*

The colour of a British rider participating in the heat of
an uphill finish on the Tour de France for the first time.

I

Icare *nm*

Icare (or 'Icarus' in English) is a term ascribed to a talented but doomed climber. He is said to have 'legs of wax and feathers' and will determinedly and repeatedly try to 'fly too close to the summit'.

In the long and glorious history of cycling, there have been many *Icares*. These days, they are, commonly, French riders whose vanity and inflated sense of self-worth lead them to consistently overestimate their own ability in the high mountains.

For every *Icare*, itching to fly off into the azure sky and leave the mass of mediocre mankind behind him, there is invariably a Daedalus: a dour, if well-meaning, *directeur sportif*, who will be warning his excitable charge about the potential hubris of misjudging his efforts on the Queen Stage.

Igloo *nm*

The 'Salle de Presse' at the Tour de France. A room kept in constant air-conditioned, chilly gloom, despite the hot splendours of a French summer outside. Peopled by troglodytes.

Imberbe *adj*

Beardless, or smooth-cheeked. Like a first-year professional.

The life of a *coureur imberbe* in the *peloton* is far from serene. While most of the indignities meted out on the youngsters revolve around the unimaginative ritual humiliations of the cyclist (mustard in the bib-shorts, barbecue sauce in the shoes, stabilising wheels fitted to the bike etc.), certain practices still exist that are designed to put hair on the chests of even the most callow and *imberbe* of youths.

For example, the Française des Jeux squad has only just abandoned its long-standing tradition that every newly signed trainee to the team must present themselves to the local gendarmerie dressed as Little Bo Peep, and report her sheep as stolen. The gendarmes on duty at the local station near Jausiers (where FDJ train) were always in on the annual joke, and would then ask them to identify their missing sheep from an impromptu sheep parade.

The last unfortunate *imberbe* to be on the receiving end of such treatment resigned on the spot, and signed instead for arch rivals AG2R the following day.

However, at the first training camp of his new team he was forced to break into Poitiers Zoo and read the whole of Stendhal's *Le Rouge et le Noir* to a cage full of meerkats.

Imbroglio *nm*

Miscounting on a circuit race and taking the victory salute an entire lap too early. Not to be confused with *gaffe*.

Immolation *nf*

Prolonged agony.

An initial stint, sometimes lasting as long as a decade, in which a rider is employed as a domestique on a lesser French team.

Immunité *nf*

Untouchable status in the *peloton*.

Some riders just get away with it. It doesn't take long to realise that, amid the hurly-burly and power politics of the *peloton*, there are a select and tiny band of riders who are given full licence to do exactly as they please. These men are said to possess *immunité*, and are spoken of in awe and reverence.

Perhaps the most infamous rider ever to claim immunity was the Swiss *rouleur* Timo Schlindl, whose greatest achievement was an unlikely solo victory in the high-summit finish in his hometown of Verbier in the 1950 Tour de France; an eyebrow-raising achievement for a stocky sprinter, to say the least.

His countryman Ferdi Kübler, who would go on to win the Tour that year, reacted with disbelief and consternation at the victory of his teammate.

'Timo is good, yes. But so too are dumplings. And they don't win bike races.'

His choice of the insult 'dumpling' (or 'Dampfknoepfli') was pointed. For Schlindl, a passionate if largely talentless amateur cyclist, had started his business career in the immediate aftermath of the Second World War, travelling around the US-occupied West German zone selling flour-based dumplings from the back of an old baker's van to American soldiers out on patrol or guarding Army facilities. The demand for Schlindl's Knoepfli was insatiable. Within a year he had hired a fleet of a dozen baker's vans, and by 1947 he was a millionaire.

By 1948, he had houses in Lausanne, Nice and London. But he was lonely and reclusive, seldom emerging during daylight hours, and virtually never seen in public. And all this at the age of twenty-four.

So it was that he returned to his childhood passion: cycling. He hired all the greats of the post-war *peloton* to train him during the winter. He paid the riders handsomely in dumplings for their efforts. The top ten riders in the world all fought each other for the next handout from the Schlindl table. They began to rely on him.

Under their tutelage, and within a year, he was ready for his first race, the Tour de France.

When he attacked at the foot of the final climb up to Verbier (on a day when the *peloton* had had to wait for him to catch up seven times already), no one was greatly surprised.

In fact, no sooner had he gone off the front than the head of the race ground to a virtual standstill, with several big-name riders forming a blockade across the road to prevent anyone from chasing Schlindl down.

They needn't have worried. He had complete *immunité*. More than half the *peloton* by now had either received free, or heavily discounted, regular parcels of freeze-dried Swiss dumplings through the post.

Chemical analysis revealed them to be stuffed with amphetamines and opiates. Schlindl dumplings are now on the list of prohibited performance-enhancing substances, as set out by the World Anti-Doping Agency.

Implant *nm*

A rarely used, extremely unreliable and expensive form of biomechanical doping, developed in New Mexico in the late 1990s, in which a rider's muscle mass is augmented with heterogenous fibres grown from the host's DNA in properly scientific-looking Petri dishes.

It is a painstaking procedure administered by men in surgical masks and sandals using Bunsen burners, pipettes and chemistry things.

Today you can probably get it on the Internet.

Inégalité *nf*

Along with a lack of brotherliness and liberty, it is generally accepted that the cycling world should be unequal.

Indeed, it is the holy grail for riders to create an environment that is decidedly unequal, tipping every advantage in one's favour. In the past, of course, this certainly resulted in the wide-scale use of performance-enhancing drugs. These days it is more nuanced.

Team Sky (see *Ciel*), although publicly espousing a policy of *accroissement marginal*, secretly abandoned the philosophy of Marginal Gains in 2013, declaring it to be 'about as useful as a bloody stepladder on the north face of the Eiger' (according to their former *directeur sportif*, the disgraced Benny Tankred, writing in his 2014 autobiography *Het was niet mijn schuld* [*It Wasn't My Fault*]).

Instead, they started to embrace the pre-existing philosophy of *inegalité*, first developed in the mid 1980s by the French team Monsieur Meuble, whose riders all benefited from free fitted kitchens for their wives. It became a matter of principle to start spoiling their riders, thus generating a self-destructive turmoil of petty jealousy among the opposing teams. It worked wonders.

As a result, Team Sky bought a fleet of personalised helicopters for each rider's transport back to the hotel after a stage, and a matching, scaled-down, but fully functional, helicopter for their children to use for visiting on rest days.

Not only that, but their riders are also given 2GB of free roaming data.

Ingratitude *nf*

Considered by most within the profession to be a mandatory prerequisite – an instinctive and complete inability to acknowledge the contribution of others. Closely related to, but not quite as valiant a sentiment as, *fierté*.

It should be noted that the celebrated quality of *ingratitude* is in stark contrast to victorious riders' public utterances. It is understood to be a necessary evil upon winning a race that one must parrot back to the press a well-rehearsed but quite disingenuous patter about how one 'couldn't have done it without all the work by the team today. They were magnificent. This is my way of repaying them.'

Such trite self-deprecation should be treated with more than a pinch of salt.

Most riders, upon fulfilling their obligations to the press, hastily return to the team bus, punch a hole in the ceiling, and holler 'Who's the fucking hero here? I'm the fucking hero!' Often, they will thrust whatever trophy they have been

111

handed on the podium at their teammates, to an accompanying cry of 'In your face!'

Then they will normally grab the microphone at the front and start to sing a wittily adapted version of the classic Queen song 'We Are The Champions', reworked so that the chorus becomes a solo 'I am the champion . . .' (pause) ' . . . of the world!'

Insaisissable *adj*

Unseizeably hard to grab hold of.

Used in cycling to describe the attempt to grapple with an inappropriate foodstuff in a musette. Like a peeled lychee, sweetbreads or a king prawn.

Intestat *adj*

Intestate.

Descriptive of the unforeseen consequences of an inexplicable and surprising capitulation.

If a rider gives up suddenly and without any possible explanation mid-race, it is often said that they surrendered *intestat*, meaning that they died on a race (not literally), without it ever becoming clear to the rest of the *peloton* what it was that they actually intended to achieve in the first place when they attacked all on their own 148 kilometres from the finish line.

Into a headwind.

Intoxication *nf*

One of cycling's vicious circles. It has two distinct definitions that are often interlinked:

(i) A state of deluded self-belief. A rider who attacks with 103 kilometres remaining, only to find themselves reeled back in with 98 kilometres remaining will often admit later to suffering from *intoxication*. This hugely overambitious *intestat* attack is often the result of riders reading all the absurdly puffed praise written about themselves on their own team's wholly unrealistic website, which famously never point out their glaring inadequacies.

(ii) A state of actual alcoholic inebriation, the unsavoury by-product of a heavy drinking session brought about by the previous day's humbling state of *intoxication* and its humiliating consequences.

Invérifiable *adj*

Pertaining to results on a rider's CV that pre-date the Internet.

Irrigation *nf*

Sweating of an overly profuse, agricultural nature.

Isabelle *nf*

Anything technical added to a bike, which is only questionably necessary.

Isobare *nf*

Drinking a solitary mini can of Heineken from the fridge in the corner of the hotel room at the very lowest point in the middle of a three-week stage race and sobbing gently, plagued by an unholy alliance of exhaustion, homesickness and guilt.

Isocèle *adj*

Isosceles. Descriptive of a breakaway of three riders, in which two of the three participants are equally strong, and the other one is a bit rubbish.

Ivoire *nm*

Illicitly gathered and illegally traded technology.

Jodler *vi*

To yodel. Or to abandon the race at the sight of a
mountain range looming ahead of you on the road.

J

Jaillir *vi*

To blurt out or gush forth. To talk without drawing breath. To gabble or spout. To gas on and on about stuff. To blather inconsequentially about whatever really. To open your gob and not stop until almost everyone has walked away or long since stopped feigning interest. To jabber.

It is the unbecoming, if seemingly uncontrollable habit of certain riders after a victory to give ridiculously long, detailed and uninteresting answers to really very simple questions, like 'What were your tactics today?' As soon as the answer begins, the interviewer knows intuitively that he/she is in it for the long haul.

'Well, at first we didn't know what to have for breakfast,' the rider often begins. 'I suggested toast, but, with one eye on the weather, it was decided that we should have porridge . . .'

Some riders consider the post-race TV interview to be the equivalent of a mission debrief after a bombing raid over enemy territory, just stopping short of unfolding a logbook and reading verbatim from their observations, using flip charts and models to illustrate some of the finer details.

However, such garrulousness is far from universal. Not all riders can be accused of *jaillir*.

The Belarusian Piotr Popov, for example, used only one word throughout his career, regardless of the circumstances, and with a total lack of consideration for the mother tongue of his interlocutor. That word was 'черника', which translates as 'bilberry'.

Jalabert *nm*

Something that is not quite what it seems to be.

Jérôme *nm*

A generic French rider, who even the French get confused for any number of other generic French riders.

Most teams, including those based in the UK, USA or Australia, but particularly in the continental cycling heartland of the Benelux countries, and of course France, will, from time to time, pad out their number by hiring a certain number of *Jérômes*.

Often these unfortunate riders will be locally well-connected (the nephew of a cement factory owner, or the brother of a director of a sportswear shop). Sometimes they will have one major honour on their CV on which they still trade, such as the white jersey in the Tour du Haut Var in 1997. But often their only defining feature is their sheer affordability.

Once or twice a year, almost like clockwork, every *Jérôme* will find himself in some three-hour-long breakaway on some televised race or other, forcing the world's TV commentators to find ever more imaginative ways of reformulating the only single fact of any interest that the particular *Jérôme*'s Wikipedia page throws up.

'There's *Jérôme* X. Interestingly, he started off his sporting career as a downhill skier.'

'As they crest the summit of the climb now, and begin to descend . . . not something you'd imagine would worry *Jérôme* X too greatly, whose early sporting education featured downhill skiing.'

'The sun has gone behind clouds for now, and there's been a noticeable drop in the temperature. That's not going to bother *Jérôme* X of course, not even if it snows. After all, he . . .'

Etc.

Jeudi *nm*

Literally, Thursday. However, *jeudi* is understood by cyclists to be shorthand for 'a day on which nothing will happen', a neutralised race, or a truce.

Any rider who has the temerity to attack after the team of the yellow jersey has declared that 'it is Thursday' risks, at best, permanent relegation to the margins of the *peloton*, and at worst, being forced at speed into a ditch full of residue from recently fertilised Breton cabbage fields.

As soon as a cry of *'Jeudi!'* goes up at the front of the race, most riders breathe a sigh of relief in the anticipation of a hassle-free ride to the finish line.

Theories abound as to the origins of this expression. Some claim that a succession of directors of the Tour de France have 'buried' their less picturesque stages on Thursdays, when the public appetite for the race is at its lowest ebb (the drudgery of the working week is unrelenting, and the week-end still some way off), and therefore the TV ratings are at their most modest. Armed with this understanding, the pro-*peloton* takes advantage of the general apathy surrounding the stage by effectively turning it into a gentle training ride.

There is some evidence to back this theory up. Research certainly indicates that hideously ugly towns like Seraing and Oyonnax only ever feature on Thursdays, although Sheffield's inclusion in 2014 on a Sunday goes a little way to disproving that particular thesis.

Others suggest, more plausibly, that the term *jeudi* was coined in homage to the Dadaist composer-cyclist Dieu Ledieu-Dieu, who used his participation in the 1927 Tour to publicise his self–founded quasi-religious cult *Pleurophantasmagie*. The main tenet of his new belief system was the introduction of the 2,000-day week, which ended on Thursdays, the day of rest for *Pleurophantasmagiciens*.

Dieu Ledieu-Dieu finished third on Stage Ten to Bayonne. On a Wednesday. The following day he disappeared.

Jongleur *nm*

A juggler.

A rider who is capable of riding for minutes on end, over many kilometres, even over cobbles or level crossings, without touching the handlebars, and often manipulating foodstuffs.

The most celebrated *jongleur* (indeed, quite possibly the only one ever recorded) was almost certainly Estoban Villa, the Colombian who completed the inaugural 1903 Tour de France in a time that was so extraordinarily slow (180 hours) that the organisation was forced, the following year, to introduce a cut-off.

It subsequently emerged that Villa had been suffering for many years from chronic lumbago, and found that he was really only comfortable sitting bolt upright on a bike. As a result, he became astonishingly good at cycling hands-free, and was able instead to perform all manner of fascinating circus tricks while riding the race. At times, he attracted more attention than the race's eventual winner Maurice Garin. The French public warmed greatly to him, and lined the roads to celebrate his passage.

Villa was photographed playing a violin, reading a book and kneading dough. He even wrote a diary, mid-race, for the newspaper *La Voix du Nord*, flourishing a pen, with a bound leather notebook and an ink well balanced on his bars.

Sadly, Villa's career was cut short a week after completing the race when he injured himself falling down the steps into the Paris Metro while trying to peel an orange on his bike.

Joujou *nm*

A laughably small bicycle, built for a very small rider. Like Richie Porte's.

Journaliste *nm*

Pejorative.

A rider who has friends in the media, openly consorts with the press in hotel lobbies, gives his phone number out to newspaper writers, blogs or generally appears on the TV more than once a year. A media tart.

Jugement *nm*

That definitive, yet curiously hard to define moment at which a rider realises they will never amount to very much.

All but the very few riders who are able to contest for the major honours, perhaps one per cent of the *peloton*, will at some point have to face up to the fact that they are simply there to make up the numbers. This grave realisation is known and feared as the dreaded *jugement*, from which there is no return.

Some rail against their destiny, and succumb to very volatile, extremely public breakdowns, as did the Spanish climber Enrique Sanchez, whose demise was as dramatic as it was humiliating.

His parents had been so certain he would win the Vuelta that they'd applied to the local council to rename their street in his honour, and lodged an application with the Catholic Church in Andalusia to turn his birthday into an annual festival. All this before young Enrique had turned thirteen.

Sadly, his career never quite unfolded as his parents had so fervently desired. His best result was in a local circuit race in Córdoba, where he took a wrong turning and accidentally cut out an 8-kilometre loop, and even then he only finished third.

His last participation in any race ended at the 1974 Tour of Catalonia, when the Guardia Civil had to talk him down from a lamppost overlooking the finishing line of Stage Three, from which he was tossing down anchovies onto the waiting crowd, shouting, 'I may not win today, but I will win all our tomorrows! See how I feed the five thousand!'

Other riders, such as five-time Tour winner Bernard Hinault, are still awaiting *jugement*. Although, in his words, 'not any time soon'.

Keirin *nm*

A motorbike rider blissfully unaware that
the entire *peloton* is slipstreaming him.

K

Kérosène *nm*

A highly motivating appearance fee paid by organisers of a bike race in the Gulf States to secure the commitment of stars of the European *peloton*.

Kimono *nm*

A poorly fitting skinsuit, provided by a less well-resourced team.

The term was first used by the foppish British time-triallist David Millar, riding for the now defunct Saunier Duval in 2007. To protest against the poor cut of his skinsuit, he painted his face white and planted two chopsticks in his lacquered hair, sticking out from his aero helmet.

Klaxon *nm*

A naive and newly qualified *directeur sportif.*

The word is derived from the tendency for fresh-faced sports directors to over-compensate for their nerves with their incessant parping of a car's horn, or klaxon. Relentless tooting of the horn is considered to be a transparent show of bravado designed to mask their own insecurities about driving a team car in a race convoy for the first time. Thus, such drivers are dismissively known as *klaxons*.

Ruud Curver, the largely anonymous Dutch ex-sprinter, was, according to many within cycling, the most notorious *klaxon*. His elevation to the rank of management within the Top-Pot Tuin Center Team of the early 1990s was short-lived but spectacular.

It ended during the first mountain stage of the 1993 Tour de Romandie (see *Euthanasie*), when Curver inexplicably found himself driving at breakneck speed the wrong way up the final climb of the day, and into the middle of the *peloton*, all the while beeping his horn, which had been fitted out to play 'The Yellow Rose of Texas'. He came to a halt just in front of a bemused Miguel Indurain.

Curver then slowly got out of the car, handed the Spanish champion his keys, and walked calmly away from the scene, pausing only to look over his shoulder as his team-issue Peugeot slipped back down the road, and over the edge of a low parapet into the valley below. He had forgotten to apply the handbrake.

Kopeck *nm*

Shady-sounding payment from a dubiously titled sponsor.

In the long, and nakedly commercial, history of professional cycling, many thousands of sponsors have come and gone. Some have been more glamorous and 'blue chip' than others. For every Jaguar and Motorola, there is a Brioche La Boulangère or Alpecin Caffeine Shampoo.

But sometimes, the very nature of the sponsor's business makes for an uncomfortable commercial proposition, which is when the riders have to sweat to earn their *kopeck*.

It was the famously avaricious (see *Grippe-sou*) French sprinter Claude Spirelli who made this expression part of cycling folklore when he publicly expounded on his personal sponsorship deal with the Union of Soviet Socialist Republics.

For his participation in the 1982 Tour de France, at the height of the Cold War, he had the Cyrillic letters CCCP controversially embroidered on all his kit, and rode a red bike, against team orders, and incurring a fine from the race direction every day. His bills were paid by Moscow.

But the contractual obligations to his unusual sponsors didn't stop there. He refused, as a matter of principle, to ride alongside any riders whose team liveries represented the interests of a capitalist institution. That, basically, meant the entire *peloton*. As a result, he either had to launch a solo attack or ensure that he was instantly dropped on every single stage.

Defending his unusual stance, when questioned by France Télévision's evening news bulletin, he uttered the now infamous phrase, 'chacun faut gagner son *kopeck*' (everyone must earn their kopeck).

Spirelli retired to Voronezh, in Russia, where he still works as a brand ambassador for a manufacturer of nerve gas and other agents of chemical warfare.

Kremlin *nm*

Paris.

Disgruntled riders, after labouring round the three weeks of the Tour de France, are often heard to refer to the final stage's showpiece finale on the Champs-Élysées as *La Place Rouge*, or 'Red Square', as if the high-ranking officials of the sports governing bodies, seated in the hospitality stands, were members of the Politburo inspecting their troops at a May Day parade.

Kryptonite *nf*

An ineffectual or pretentious foodstuff. One that will sabotage a rider's chances by being almost inedible.

Team doctors face an uphill battle convincing their charges that, at a mitochondrial level, their bodies are best nourished by feasting on puffin-egg-white omelette and caraway surprise. For many riders, their day has effectively ended before they've even stepped on a bike, so weakened are they by their *kryptonite* breakfast.

Modern cuisine is routinely blamed for underperformance on the bike. Recently, especially among the better-funded World

Tour teams, there has been a vogue for hiring post-modern Scandinavian chefs, whose culinary universe is centred around the humble beetroot.

There is nothing that these gifted kitchen-based artisans are not able to serve up from a combination of watercress, anchovy, quinoa and pomegranate seeds. Riders, particularly those of an older generation who remember the halcyon days of unfettered spaghetti Bolognese consumption, often react badly when faced with a plate of poached parsley roots in a tangerine jus.

Things reached a head during the 2012 Tour de France, when the entire Trek Factory Racing team, led by a furious Fabian Cancellara, threw their dinner of artichoke consommé over their chef and traipsed out of their hotel to the fast-food establishment next door. The mutiny became known as 'The Battle of the Buffalo Grill'.

Lancer *vtr*

Never to test positive for performance-enhancing drugs.

L

Labrador *nm*

An unexpected obstacle that suddenly appears on the race route, unseating the rider.

This is a relatively recent expression, only dating back to 2007. While the most notorious *action de labrador* was Marcus Burghardt's collision during that year's Tour with an eponymous hound, the history of random collisions is as old as the race itself. From express trains to beach balls, small children to sheep, there is no telling what moving object might suddenly present itself as an obstacle.

The earliest recorded *labrador* took the shape of a French military observation balloon, tethered near the race route of the 1914 Tour de France in Belfort to spy on German troop movements. For some unknown reason the balloon, complete with its three-man crew, rapidly lost altitude and ended up landing on top of the *peloton* on their approach to the finish line.

Scenes of chaos ensued, as dozens of riders were caught underneath the extensive, flaccid canvas canopy, and struggled frantically to get free with their bicycles. Eventually, as several riders lost their bearings, fights broke out, and punches were thrown, albeit all under the cover of the deflated material. The crowd were delighted by the scenes.

A German cameraman, who happened to be on the route to film the race, captured the whole event. However, the footage was later put to use for propaganda purposes in a Germany that was readying itself for war. The film, titled *Die Tour de Farce*, proved hugely popular, provoking great hilarity among cinema-goers up and down the Second Reich, as it confirmed their deeply held suspicions that their Gallic neighbours were inherently foolish and ineffectual, and that beating them on the field of battle would be a cinch.

Two weeks later Germany declared war on France. Ironically, some years later, France won.

Lapin *nm*

A rabbit. A nervy, minor rider, prone to wildly impulsive, quite ineffectual riding.

No single character better suits this description than André Lapierre, the man whose very frailty and exuberance on a bike gave rise to the expression itself.

His defining characteristic, as a rider, was his fruitless daily attempts to get in the breakaway. But, nervy by nature, he could never wait until the conditions were right for an attack, and chose instead to launch himself excitedly off the front every time the flag dropped and the race began.

After several years of trying to get in the day's *échappée* without a single success, it became customary for the *peloton* simply to let him go for a few kilometres, laughing as he disappeared towards the horizon (treatment that echoed the earlier career of Guy Parfouffe [see *Babiller*]).

Then they would reel him in, and, with the *lapin* sinking like a stone back through the bunch, his job done, they could begin the race in earnest.

Despite, or perhaps because of his ineffectualness, he was well-liked in the ranks of professional cycling. Indeed, on the last stage of his final Tour de France in 1996, he was allowed to ride off at the front of the race and soak up the warm applause of the crowd. After Lapierre's famous solo '*lap-in* of honour' around the Champs-Élysées, the French newspaper *Le Parisien* printed the memorable headline '*OH LA LA! LE LAPIN LAPIERRE!*'

This headline then became the title of a short-lived game show on French TV, hosted by Lapierre, which involved members of the public racing miniature clowns' bikes against celebrities around a greyhound track in pursuit of a rabbit.

Lattis *nm*

Lathing, or lathwork. The habitual shaving off of virtually invisibly small layers from a surface area in order to save weight (see *Ajustage*).

The practice of *lattis* was taken to extraordinary lengths by Japan's Akio Hamasaki, whose fully denuded body was also scrubbed with pumice stone every morning to remove the dead and dying skin from its surface. Hamasaki retired from the sport after failing to recover from an infection in the self-inflicted wounds, resulting from his attempts to embed cleats into the fleshy pad of his foot – a procedure he believed would relieve him of the need to ride with the extra weight of shoes (see *Gramophone*).

Lèchefrite *nf*

A dripping pan. An unglamorous event. A late-season race. An afterthought in the cycling calendar.

Racing in October is considered by the majority of the *peloton* to be both tiresome and totally unrewarding. All the Classics are over, the Grand Tours have been raced and the World Championships contested. Most of the *peloton* are already on holiday, negotiating new contracts on the beachfront at Dubai.

However, some unfortunates are sent to places like China and Taiwan in order to go through the motions of a bike race.

Winning in parts of the world that are considered unimportant by the haughty Eurocentric world of the professional *peloton* is like not winning at all. It is like licking the fat from the leftovers of a meal. Like dining from a *lèchefrite*.

No one won more *lèchefrites* than Mario Cipollini's unheralded older brother Mirco. Rarely seen at any European races, he nonetheless amassed an extraordinary number of stage wins in contests such as the now defunct The Three Days of Grozny, and the no-longer-raced Ulan Bator–Darkhan–Ulan Bator.

Indeed, his remarkable 22-stage winning streak in the sadly lapsed Tour of Artem was commemorated in 2000 by the erection of a statue on a hillside outside the Palace of Sports in Vladivostok. It was stolen in 2010, and has since been replaced by a mobile phone mast.

Longueur *nf*

Since professional bike racing is defined by the powerful, yet abstract concept of length, there is considered to be no greater philosophical value than *longueur*.

To enhance our understanding of this difficult concept, the Sorbonne-based Professor of Semantics and Abstract Mathematics, and runner-up in the 1995 Paris–Tours, Michel Sankowitz, famously defined the true value of *longueur* in his 1997 treatise 'The Empirico-Spiritual Length of Cycling' as being 'a priori in advance of, in negative relation defined by, without tangential reference to, and in dimensional respect of all reason, inasmuch as the dynamic contained within are wholly subject to applicable parameters understood within said framework, such that it may be seen in terms of the following formulation: *Longueur* > Valour * Portionality'.

This definition of the true meaning of *longueur* is widely understood among the *peloton* to be the most cogent, although recently, a separate school of thought within the younger riders on the American Cannondale squad has developed.

These riders, known collectively as the 'Situationists of the Saddle', have contested that Sankowitz's conception is probably unreliable to within a likelihood of 'around about seven'.

Lotto *nm*

Fatalism. Not to be confused with *destin*.

There is a certain inevitability in a long cycling career, that at some point every rider will end up riding for a team sponsored by a national, or even regional, lottery.

This contract will entail wearing a gaudy, unlovely kit (see *Arlequin*), and posing for photographs in which he is asked to throw hundreds of fake bank notes at the camera, jump into the air with both hands outstretched in celebration, or pop fake champagne corks.

This bitter reality is, by and large, simply accepted as unavoidable by the cycling community, who are known for their phlegmatic approach to life in general. Every cyclist riding for a *lotto* team may throw envious glances in the direction of their colleagues who are employed by a team sponsored by a famous bike brand, sports cars, satnav or satellite television station.

But deep down they know that what goes around comes around, and that one day their number will come up (see *Hospice*).

Marron *nm*

A chestnut. An overenthusiastic, inebriated fan,
who has chosen to climb a tree in order to watch
the passage of a bicycle race.

M

Macadamisage *nm*

The embedding of a smattering of tiny, sharp fragments of tarmac into the skin of one's buttocks after crashing on a descent from a mountain.

Maillot *nm*

A jumper. Everyone knows that.

Marennes *nf*

Inspired by the Marennes oyster, this term applies to riders who look formidably tough on the outside, but are soft to the point of putrefaction on the inside.

Marketing *nm*

Sponsor-friendly membership of a pointless, doomed break-away on a stage of a bicycle race on live television.

Meccano *nm*

The rather less expensive equipment supplied by a rider's national squad, as opposed to his/her trade team, on occasions such as the Olympic Games when they are on international duty. It is not very good.

Mégaphone *nm*

Jens Voigt.

Mensualité *nf*

The ability of an otherwise indolent rider to post, on average, one result per month of sufficient merit that his contract isn't terminated.

Métissage *nm*

Crossbreeding.

The ungainly look of a two-man escape featuring a duo of riders from different teams, one of whom is significantly taller and more muscular than the other. The result of such a mismatch can only, it is argued, be ill-fated.

The aesthetics of cycling normally dictate that a pair of riders working together in an attack should be physically evenly matched. It offends the eye for it to be otherwise. Certain old-school *directeurs sportifs* will even order their charges to withdraw from the move if it is considered that their ill-matching physiologies are so unaesthetic as to be seen to be bringing the sport into disrepute.

'Yes, he could have won the stage,' recalled the great French *directeur sportif* Sylvain Pellicule, when recounting the Queen Stage of the 1985 Tour, 'but at what cost? My rider was a risible midget, a miserable speck of a man on the wheel of that beastly West German hulk. And the fruit of that union could only have been a gross disfigurement, a horrible *métissage*, for which our beautiful sport would only have suffered. I had no choice but to order him to desist. France demanded it. Cycling demanded it. Honour compelled me to act.'

Pellicule had driven the team car up to the breakaway and ordered his rider, Henri Talent, to withdraw, with a wave of a white lace handkerchief, and weeping bitter tears, all of which were seen by a captivated television audience.

Michelin *adj*

Out of condition. Descriptive of the temporary body shape assumed by riders returning to training after a few weeks off over Christmas.

Mignon *adj*

A patronising adjective used to describe footling victories in any given race outside of the European cycling heartland. *Une victoire mignonne* would customarily be celebrated on Canadian or Algerian soil and most certainly not in France, Italy or Belgium.

Minéralogiste *nmf*

A rare breed of rider who can tell simply by looking at the hue, density and compactness of the tarmac which country they are in.

The best *minéralogists*, men such as the German domestique for Giant-Alpecin, Arno Grau, boast that they can not only identify the region from its tarmac, but, more exactly, the precise identity of the road in question. Since his sudden retirement in 2013, and amid rumours of 'extraordinary rendition', Grau is widely believed to have been working for the CIA, deciphering drone-gathered intelligence in Pakistan.

Minimiser *vtr*

To downplay one's chances. To remain obdurately and unnecessarily gloomy in any given race (see also *Vaticiner*).

'I'd be happy with thirty-second' was the constant refrain of mediocre Czech sprinter Havel Knak during his one and only

Tour de France participation in 2004. He was making his debut in the race at the mature age of thirty-two.

To everyone's delight, he finished the very last stage in thirty-second place, having made the same prediction every day, but until that point never having managed anything higher than thirty-sixth. There was a suspicion that several of the riders ahead of him, having made a lightning-fast calculation at the number of riders ahead of them, slowed in the final few metres of the Champs-Élysées stage in order to allow the popular Czech to sprint for his beloved thirty-second.

The Czech National Championships still feature a special 'Knak' jersey for the rider who finished the previous edition in thirty-second place, although it is not recognised by the UCI.

Sadly, Knak never wore the jersey named after him, and retired in 2006.

Mistral *nm*

Originating from the cold wind that blows from the North, this term refers to anything anti-Mediterranean, or anything unpleasant and unwelcome that originates in grey European climates. Like brown bread and parsnips (see *Hanséatique*).

A highly flexible term, applicable equally to unnecessarily muscular and undeniably dull riders from Scandinavian countries (*coureurs de Mistral*), as well as onerous participations in low-key and terrifyingly inclement Belgian races such as Roeselare–Brussels–Roeselare–Brussels–Roeselare or the Dutch Food Valley Classic, and making personal appearances for sponsors with drab headquarters on the out-skirts of uninspiring towns like Hannover.

Momification *nf*

The embalming in extra layers required for racing in early-season Belgian one-day races.

Monastère *nm*

The suddenly serious atmosphere in a team hotel on the morning of a particularly brutal race.

On such occasions, with the wind howling around the hotel and the heavy rain battering against the windows, riders are seen awake at ungodly hours, shuffling slowly along corridors and across courtyards, mouthing barely audible prayers to no one in particular.

In extreme cases, riders have been known to gather in the pre-dawn gloom of the breakfast room, dressed only in their hotel bath robes, with complimentary disposable slippers on their feet, and incant in Latin the list of television channels available in their rooms.

Montagnard *nm*

A mountain dweller. A rider who, having grown up in the mountains, is unfazed by sudden changes of temperature, landslides, blue-coloured rivers, thin air, cowbells, molten cheese-based cuisine, upper-middle-class British families with second homes in the Alps and the constant thudding of helicopter rotor blades in the distance.

Montgolfière *nf*

An overly ornate helmet design, that nonetheless gives an impression of weightlessness.

Moutarde *nf*

Any race that begins, ends or passes through the city of Dijon.

Mugissement *nm*

The animalistic low-frequency bellowing unconsciously emitted by a rider in the final throes of exertion en route to placing no higher than fifteenth on any given stage.

A higher-placed finish is widely understood to result in a higher-frequency groan, and is routinely produced by riders of greater capacity and earning potential.

Mugissement, however, is exclusively associated with the kind of pained and fearful booming emitted by cattle when disembarking their transports at the gates of an abattoir.

Myrtille *nf*

A whortleberry. Commonly used to refer to a raised saddle sore.

Neutron *nm*

A tiny rider capable of producing sudden
and astonishingly explosive power.

N

Napoléon *nm*

Any grotesquely over-celebrated French rider of slight stature, whose achievements were, at best, questionable, and whose career ultimately unravelled dramatically on a field somewhere near Waterloo in a Belgian classic.

Narval *nm*

A virtually extinct rider equipped with a mysterious yet ultimately pointless adornment akin to the 'tusk' of a narwhal.

Most commonly, this is used to describe the dwindling number of riders who still believe that there is a physiological advantage to be gained from those white strips which adhere to the outside of the nose, and are supposed to prise open the airways. However, the same epithet was also well suited to riders who, during the late twentieth century, rode time trials in absurdly long, tapered aero helmets.

Navette *nf*

A shuttle service. The hard-working team of a particularly accident-prone leader.

These riders are indefatigably working for their leader, a racer who is repeatedly dropping out of the back of the *peloton* as a result of some mechanical problem, or after a light fall, only for his entire team to be sent back to the convoy of cars in order to shepherd him back up to the front of the race.

Négatif *adj*

Lucky (see *Positif*).

Négligé *adj*

Descriptive of kit that shows sign of wear and tear.

Like socks that are supposed to be white, but have gone a bit grey in the wash, or a helmet with a scratch. Or scuffed shoes. Normally associated with teams from Portugal and the Republic of Ireland. Never with the immaculately turned-out French teams, except those poorly-funded outfits from Normandy, and parts of the Auvergne.

Niche *nf*

A unique specialisation in some terribly obscure aspect of racing culture, so narrow and specific as to be virtually ignored by the rest of the cycling world.

Certain riders are depended upon within their teams for their rare ability to ride in fog, whereas others are prized for their prowess at taking left-handed hairpins on wet descents. There have been those who excel at passing châteaux at speed, whereas other are at their best, for whatever reason, when the race is routed past fields of standing cattle.

The most celebrated *niche* of all was believed to be that of Alexandre Dinde, a lead-out rider from Bayonne, who would only be selected for races in towns which had, at some point, hosted Ultravox concerts. The reasons for this particular specialisation were never divulged.

Nœud *nm*

A knot. The inextricable tangle of riders in intimate contact with each other and each other's body parts, left on the road in the aftermath of a mass pile-up (see *Picasso*).

Normal *adj*

Completely conforming to expectations. A philosophical term that expresses the intellectual, spiritual, physiological and tactical certainty with which an experienced professional cyclist approaches his/her trade.

The absence of anything that can surprise or alarm a pro is the hallmark of maturity in a bike rider. Hence, it would be described as *normal* if a hailstorm erupted out of clear blue skies in the middle of summer to disrupt the closing kilometres of a transitional stage in the Camargue.

It is also decidedly *normal* that, on occasions, entire teams of French riders get blown into a ditch by freak gusts of wind, or certain riders succumb to equally sudden and bewilderingly voluble bouts of gastroenteritis. *Normal*.

Likewise, any kind of volcanic eruption, strike action by agricultural workers or impromptu guerrilla action by partisans of any persuasion might be greeted with a shrug of the shoulders and the downplayed assertion that *'c'est normal'*. Nothing surprises a true pro.

The only intrusion into their closely marshalled lives that a modern professional does not consider to be *normal* is the lack of decent coffee at the team hotel.

This can instantly enrage an otherwise sanguine athlete, and lead them to carry out acts of surprising violence on crockery at breakfast buffets for which the team management has to pick up the bill. Most modern agents have a crockery clause written into their riders' contracts.

Notaire *nm*

A stickler for the rules, a grey man, an unromantic rider.

Finnish sprinter Jari Maikennennen, runner-up on Stage Three of the 1993 Tour (recognised throughout the cycling world as the dullest on record (see *Caque*)), was the most celebrated (tolerated) *notaire* of them all. He was well known in the *peloton* for shouting out the paragraph and rule number from the UCI Regulations of Road Racing that he perceived was being infringed during a bunch sprint.

Thus, he was often heard to bellow out '2.3.06!', swiftly followed by 'riders shall be strictly forbidden to deviate from the lane they selected when launching into the sprint and, in so doing, endangering others!'

He wasn't very popular. In 2003, upon his retirement, he accepted a position in a firm of Finnish compliance consultants, for whom he continues to work, principally contracted to clients in the domestic telecoms market. He lives in Töölö, near Helsinki. With his mother.

Notre-Dame *nf*

A rider whose lesser pace forms an impediment to the flow of the *peloton*, causing it to split into two halves in order to circumnavigate the slow-moving obstacle.

Seen from the air, this curiously beautiful phenomenon resembles the Île de la Cité in Paris, on which the

Notre-Dame Cathedral stands, and around which the River Seine flows.

Nougat *nm*

The French equivalent of Marmite.

A rider, a team, or a race that divides opinion, in much the same way as a bar of the Montélimar-based, overly sticky sweet. Anything described as *nougat* is both saccharine and at the same time extremely difficult to enjoy.

The Tour de Suisse, for instance, has traditionally been known as La Course de Nougat, as it features stunning mountainous countryside, complete with picturesque cattle flaunting huge bells underneath their chins, lax taxation arrangements and chocolate-box villages of timbered houses.

But it is invariably shrouded in icy rain, largely devoid of spectators who aren't entirely neutral and features accommodation in a string of gloomy hotels that only cater for pork and dumpling lovers. Most riders abandon after the first day in the mountains, claiming dementia.

The winner of the Tour de Suisse is, of course, given a prize of his body-weight in Toblerone, a confectionary that is famously nougat-based, only adding to the ambiguity.

Nous *pron*

Us.

As opposed to them. The term by which the cycling fraternity differentiate themselves from the rest of the population
of the planet.

Novembre *nm*

A yearned-for absence of effort, taking its name from the
only month during which most pros can take a complete
break from riding.

Novembre can also be used to describe an easier day on a race.
Or indeed anything that isn't too taxing. Completing a reasonably simple Suduko during a rest day, for instance, might
be considered *un novembre*. So too would be the act of watching an unusually comprehensible episode of the reasonably
confusing TV series *Lost*.

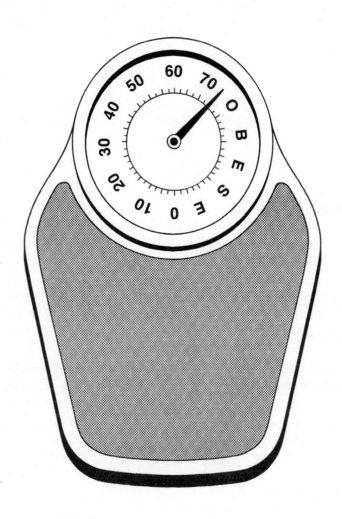

Obèse *adj*

73 kg.

Oblitération *nf*

Competitive dinner time during a stage race.

Former T-Mobile super-domestique Andreas Klöden still holds the World Kilo record for the consumption of a kilogram of tagliatelle after Stage Thirteen of the 2003 Tour de France.

It was a verified standard-width egg-and-flour-based flat noodle with 20 grams of parmesan and a teaspoon of olive oil. He finished the meal in 13.82 seconds, loading the pasta into a staggeringly economical four twisted forkfuls, an average of just under three and a half seconds per mouthful.

Occiput *nm*

Literally, the back of a head.

But figuratively, any object in the field of vision with which a rider becomes unreasonably fixated to the point of loathing during a six-hour bike race. Like a tiny nick in the handlebar tape or a visible spot on the end of one's nose, an *occiput* can madden to the point of distraction.

Five-time Tour de France champion Bernard Hinault was said to have a particularly unbearable *occiput*, famously described by his great rival Greg LeMond as 'squat, flat and intolerably smug'.

Ongulé *adj*

Ungulate, hoofed. Pertaining to a clumsy, heavy pedal stroke.

Opérette *nf*

An affectionate term, coined by the French press, for a race of limited consequence, but considerable entertainment. The light opera of the cycling world.

Such a race will often feature gently satisfying comic relief, in the shape of an amusing collision with some local wildlife, mild betrayal, as a rather feeble team leader is undermined by a treacherous attack from one of his lieutenants, as well as a suggestion of menace from a pantomime villain, often in the form of a rider from the former Soviet Union. Or some Italian bloke.

Orchestration *nf*

The division, along orchestral lines, of the *peloton* into different functions.

Fierce disagreements and resentments can arise from the perception that a rider has been falsely designated. Nonetheless, even in the contemporary *peloton*, everyone knows his place.

Very few riders can genuinely look forward to the status of trumpets or violins. For many, a place within the ranks of the clarinets is the very height of their ambition, while other still lowlier practitioners simply aspire to taking their seat alongside the trombones, piccolos or even the cors anglais. Nobody wants to be a timpani or a tambourine, the very worst of them all.

Impressionist composer Claude-Achille Debussy, a keen cycling fan in his latter years (see *Decrescendo*), was the first to draw these comparisons, in his celebrated *Suite pour un Peloton*, itself the inspiration for Benjamin Britten's *The Young Person's Guide to the Orchestra*.

Debussy's work begins with a quotation from Henri Desgrange himself, the founding father of the Tour de France:

> You, dear rider, are nothing but a hollow vessel, a brass tube, a horse hair bow, a giant beating stick. But I am your creator. See how I make you move, wildly, with passion, and at once in quiet contemplation with each sacred flick of my conductor's baton.

Orica *nm*

Any act of vandalism resulting in damage to the infrastructure of the Tour de France.

Believed to be a reference to the Orica GreenEDGE team bus getting stuck under the finishing arch on Stage One of the 2013 Tour de France (see *Animateur*).

Origami *nm*

The art of enduring an exceptionally boring team briefing.

This is achieved by folding and refolding the paper, on which the profile of the day's stage is printed. Most riders find it hard to concentrate on tactical details, and tend to stop listening. Besides, the *directeur sportif* will probably repeat himself on a daily basis. If it's a sprinter's stage, it'll be something about 'getting so-and-so to the front with a kilometre to go'. If it's a mountain stage it'll be something about 'getting so-and-so to the foot of the climb nicely placed on the wheel of the favourites'.

Racing a bike's really not very complicated.

And besides, if you fold the paper twice in the middle, the second time at an angle, then fold the top third at 45 degrees to the remaining portion, and fold again into equal thirds, it looks a bit like a small hat.

Osmose *nf*

The ability to absorb fluids through one's skin. Certain riders have semi-permeable membranes instead of tattoos. This serves them well when it rains.

Most notable among these was the Luxembourg climber Charley Nebel, who won the King of the Mountains competition on the 1983 Tour de France.

He thrived in the inclement weather that summer, throwing away his water bottles at the first hint of rain or even drizzle. Through the Alps, over the Massif Central, and into the Pyrenees, during which there was not a single day without some form of precipitation, Nebel was never once observed drinking from a *bidon*. He simply *osmosé* the water.

The extra weight lost on the climbs from riding without full bottles proved decisive in his victory.

Eyewitness accounts from the post-Tour party, however, at which Nebel celebrated his success by downing a bottle of Château Pétrus in one, recount seeing him 'beaded in tiny drops of bright red sweat, from his brow to the nape of his neck, as if the very surface of his skin had become the polka-dot he had so valiantly defended'.

Otage *nm*

A single rider from one team in a small breakaway containing numerous riders all from another.

This term also refers to Jean-Paul Terrebrulé, who was actually taken hostage on the 1931 Tour de France by opportunistic Spanish bandits near Andorra. He was only released several weeks later, upon payment of a ransom of a haunch of smoked venison and a pair of leather gardening gloves. There was a reason for this specific request – Terrebrulé ran a smoked-game and glove export business.

Far from expressing gratitude on his release, he was incensed that the payment to his hostage takers had been authorised at all. More than anything, he detested wastage. He sacked his brother-in-law from his position on the board, charging him with embezzlement.

To this day, characters in the bunch who display tendencies that are deemed to be petulant or lacking in generosity are often referred to as *otages*.

Oto-rhino-laryngologiste *nmf*

A rider who suffers with tedious predictability from complaints of the ear, nose and throat.

He understands the cause of such ailments, and is widely read on the subject. Nevertheless, he is powerless to ward off infection, and is always the first rider on any team to succumb. Seemingly, nothing will stem the flow of his perpetually running nostrils.

Ourlet *nm*

A hem. The delicate, decorative outer fringe of a bunched *peloton*, in which the edges are exposed to sudden narrowings of the road, and the sharpest gradients into corners. The main protagonists are normally buried within the heart of the bunch, flanked by inexperienced and less highly rated riders.

Thus 'to ride the hem', or *courir à l'ourlet*, is generally understood as a dismissive term, descriptive of naive riding.

Picasso *nm*

The aftermath of a crash involving a number of riders, particularly when eyes and arms and necks and fingers end up bent and distorted like a work of Cubist art (see *Nœud* and *Van Gogh*).

P

Paganisme *nm*

Certain disruptive and bizarre practices that do not accord with accepted norms in cycling.

Recent examples of *paganisme* include flagrant disregard for conversations that revolve endlessly around the quality of Italian coffee (Chris Froome), non-participation in sparsely attended and unpleasant regional early-season French stage races (Chris Froome) and coming from Africa (Chris Froome).

Panache *nm*

Riding with doomed flamboyance, conscious of the need to renew one's contract.

Panda *nm*

A finisher on a muddy edition of Paris–Roubaix. Full *panda* status is only achieved at the point at which his/her shades are removed.

Parachute *nm*

An unzipped rain cape on a descent.

Pavé *nm*

A cobblestone. And steak, weirdly.

The *Pavé de pavé* refers to the cobbled Arenberg Forest stretch of Paris–Roubaix, which routinely needs hosing down after the passage of the race to wash away the blood and flecks of buttock, thigh, calf and tricep.

Peloton *nm*

Platoon.

Oliver Stone is a keen cycling fan, and his cinematography reflects his passions.

Peloton d'exécution *nm*

A firing squad, or the US Postal Team of Lance Armstrong (see *Astronaute*).

Peste *nf*

The Plague.

Any illness that is undoubtedly worse than any other illness as suffered by other riders, who are obviously not as ill as the particular rider in question.

If a rider acquires the unwelcome reputation for repeated days missed through illness, they will also be assumed to be suffering from *la peste*, and as a result will have to carry a bell around the corridors of the team hotel. They will also find mysterious chalk markings above the door frame of their room, and a cedar chest placed in their room, along with sprigs of mint and pennyroyal for the safekeeping of the bacillus-infected pestilent kit.

In extreme cases, a rider with *la peste* will be banished to the annexe of the Campanile hotel for six months, or until the day of their death (see the case of Ronny Heslop under *Haire*), at which point their personal effects, and the annexe itself, shall be razed to the ground.

Pétillant *adj*

Crackling, sparkling, bubbly, vacuous, inane, transparent.

Un coureur pétillant is an overpriced, overrated rider who looks the part (wonderfully structured hair, a permanent Dubai tan and gleaming teeth), but lacks proper substance and body. Like Pomagne.

Phare *nm*

A lighthouse.

An overly upright, very tall, possibly gangly rider, whose exaggeratedly extended head emerges, beacon-like, from the *peloton*, and can be used as an orientation point by riders navigating their way through the bunch. It helps the general visibility of the *phare* in question if he rides for a team sponsored by a manfacturer of garish, neon-coloured helmets.

Philosophe *nmf*

A rider who tends towards verbosity, and talks of the sport of professional cycling in terms that are not generally understood by his less eloquent, more academically limited peers, but are lapped up by members of the press (see *Baudelairien*).

The original, and best remembered, *philosophe* of the *peloton* was the École des Beaux-Arts-educated aesthete and *rouleur* Artur Delacroix, the winner of the 1951 Paris–Camembert and an honorary doctorate from the University of Leuven.

A collection of his most famous utterings about the sport he loved was published in 1958 under the title *Ceci n'est pas un vélo*, and featured such well-known aphorisms as, 'Attention must be paid to the application of one's feet relative to the pedal. For in that attitude lies the highest good and the path to happiness', and, 'If cycling did not exist, it would be necessary to invent it', as well as, 'Cycling must be understood backwards. But it must be ridden forwards'.

Mark Cavendish is widely acknowledged to be the *peloton*'s contemporary *philosophe*. He regularly dispenses such bon mots as, 'Cycling's fucking hard'.

Piaf *nf*

A nickname given to any rider who cannot see fault in their own performance. A rider who regrets nothing.

Picardie *nf*

An onerous race of regional importance to the sponsors, but of no sporting significance.

As luck would have it, these races tend to be in Picardie, a region of northern France best known for not being as interesting as Normandy.

Pie *nf*

A magpie, or a thief.

Not, as one might assume, a thief of actual things, more a purloiner of ideas.

Traditionally, a *pie* will sidle up to the road captain or team leader of another outfit, and eavesdrop as tactics are discussed. Armed with this stolen knowledge, a *pie* under team orders would simply relay it back to their *directeur sportif*, risking interception by another *pie*.

However, there have always been a number of freelance *pies*, who, once in receipt of confidential tactical information, make their misappropriated horde available on the open market to the highest bidder. The aspiring *pie* must also be able to discern a genuine tactical conversation from a falsely broadcast bluff, designed to throw the opposition off on the wrong scent.

Equally, there are still certain less-than-scrupulous fake magpies, or *pies fausses*, who are simply charlatans trying to hawk invented intel, with no actual talent for eavesdropping. They do not last long, and are generally considered to be beneath contempt, while the best of the genuine magpies or *pies vraies* are treated with awe and respect, as if they were witchdoctors with a miracle cure.

As early as 1905, attempts were made to industrialise the information-gathering industry within the sport, with the widespread distribution throughout the *peloton* of the Tour de France of the new-fangled Oreillette device, a highly portable, discreet ear trumpet fashioned from brass and sold by the famous Saint-Étienne supplier of cycling hardware Manufacture d'Armes Française.

This was a short-lived fad and it lost currency when it became impossible for any conversation of any description, however innocent, to be conducted without the sudden extraction of a hundred ear trumpets by all riders in the immediate surroundings.

This widespread, and highly visible, manifestation of information gathering was the subject of a coruscating editorial in *L'Auto* newspaper, edited by Henri Desgrange, the man in charge of the Tour, who described the ear trumpets as looking like the 'horns of the Devil himself, spreading hatred and fear, and bringing disgrace on the Tour de France, itself the last bulwark of Christian morality against the godless swill of modernity'.

In more recent times, extreme cases have been rumoured of certain teams employing riders specifically for their technical know-how and skills in subterfuge and espionage. Sometimes, whole squads have been assembled for just that purpose, betraying the obsessive state of paranoia that infected cycling during the heyday of the EPO era.

Indeed, the Motorola team of the early 1990s used to send their riders out with adhesive micro-bugging devices in their back pockets along with their flapjack, which would be distributed among the convoy of rival team cars as Motorola riders navigated their way back into the *peloton* after seeming to suffer a puncture. But being made by Motorola, the transmitters either broke, wouldn't switch on or ran out of battery almost instantly.

Team Radio Shack, Lance Armstrong's (see *Astronaute*) team before his final retirement, fared no better. Their stuff just snapped.

Piège à éléphant *nm*

An elephant trap. A three-man breakaway on mountainous terrain, comprising two diminutive Basque climbers and one hefty Dutch all-rounder. Not to be confused with other ill-balanced breakaways (see *Souricière*).

Pieuvre *nf*

Octopus. A venomous rider, with a distinct beak and a bewildering, scuttling motion, who can squeeze through the unlikeliest of gaps.

Pilate *nm*

A rider who abdicates personal responsibility at every turn, and is overly attentive to hand hygiene, taking every opportunity to wash them, especially after a nature break or before a feed zone.

Piranha *nm*

An inconsiderable, often Portuguese-speaking, rider, who in himself poses little threat, but when placed into a team (or 'shoal') of equally inconsiderable riders, can represent a significant challenge, one which could even end in a fatality.

Pistolet (à eau) *nm*

A water pistol. Or a rider who cannot wait until the end of the neutralised section before stopping to urinate. (See *Chameau.*)

Plage *nf*

The tipping point (see *Jugement*).

The point of no return. A dangerous, wonderful, furiously powerful temptation to give up. Descriptive of a state of mind far removed from a bike race.

Philosophically, mythologically speaking, this is the 'anti-cycling' – an imagined sun-kissed beach, accompanied by the gentle rhythm of crashing waves and distant delighted cries of happy children.

A rider is said to be *sur la plage* when he can no longer cope with the terrible rigours of professional cycling, and, mid-race, freewheels gently to the side of the road, a fixed, absent smile playing across his weary features, and steps off. No amount of furious berating from the foul-tempered *directeur sportif*, pulling up alongside in his team car with the window wound down and obscenities spewing forth from within, will persuade the afflicted rider to climb back on to his bike and resume the race.

Later at the team hotel, the rider's absence from the dinner table will be discussed in hushed, furtive tones.

'Où est Jean?'

'Jean?' And then the terrible answer that awakens a powerful fear in all riders, no matter how experienced, 'Jean est *sur la plage.*'

Every rider in this cursed sport is only a single, simple, beautiful thought away from joining Jean on the beach.

Platane *nm*

A rider renowned for his capacity for recovering from crashes.

This is thought to refer to the almost magical ability of the humble plane tree (*platane*) to shed and regenerate bark, in much the same manner the skin grows back over a graze.

The Eritrean Gebre Afwerki is known throughout the cycling world as the most fabled *platane* after his stunning recovery from a terrible crash on the 2015 Tour de France, during which he lost, according to Australian sports director Gary Mitchell, 'half, or even two-thirds of his arse'. Remarkably, the next day he showed no sign of any abrasion.

It subsequently emerged that Afwerki, unable to get comfortable in his bed that night, had opted to sleep on the lawn outside his room at the Troyes Nord Balladins hotel. It was only when he woke at first light that he realised he had chosen to fall asleep directly underneath a mature plane tree.

He also didn't realise that there was an irrigation system embedded in the lawn that was timed to start watering the grass at 5.40 a.m. His rude awakening was captured by CCTV, and the footage found its way onto social media in the form of a 'comic' Vine.

#NakedCyclist briefly trended worldwide until it was superseded by #YouveBeenTangoed (promoted tweet).

Positif *adj*

Unlucky. (See *Négatif*.)

Postal *adj*

Inspired by Lance Armstrong's (see *Astronaute*) US Postal team, this term can simply be applied to any cycling endeavour successfully executed 'by whatever means it takes'.

Poudrière *nf*

A gunpowder factory, or a team packed with attacking intent.

The briefly exciting, financially unstable and always incendiary Italian outfit Team Kappa came to define a hyper-aggressive riding style that was as frustrating to watch as it was almost entirely ineffective.

The original *poudrière* (a term first used by *L'Équipe* to describe Kappa's baffling, explosive antics in the final few kilometres of 1977's Paris–Roubaix, which resulted in six of their number crashing into farms, and the other two hitting farmers) was frequently known to launch every rider, one by one, off the front of a full-blooded chase towards a bunch sprint.

They had no intention of actually winning the stage. They simply wanted to make money. Not one of them lasted more than a few seconds before being caught again, but it did guarantee the team exposure on TV during the only bit of the race that people actually bothered watching. As a result of their one-dimensional tactics, the space for sponsors' logos on the front of their helmets and on their shoulders was sold at a premium, whereas their jerseys never attracted advertisers for the empty sections on their backsides.

Briefly, the rest of the *peloton* tried to copy this financially astute tactic, and Kappa found themselves accompanied in their lone, fruitless attacks, by half the bunch. The net effect was that Kappa's tactic was simply negated by the sheer numbers of riders trying to pull the same stunt.

As a result, everyone just gave up and things went back to normal. The original *poudrière* disappeared as quickly as it had materialised.

Several teams have tried, in recent years, to pick up where Kappa left off, including Bretagne-Séché Environnement, who managed to get a man in every breakaway of every day of every race in 2014. Or at least, that's what they told their sponsor, who never actually checked.

Priseur *nm*

A taker of snuff, or a rider banned for the use of 'recreational drugs'.

Prisme *nm*

A confusing section of road, with poor or misleading signage, that leads to the race being split into a number of different directions, in a process akin to the refraction of light through a prism.

The most infamous *prisme* in modern racing happened during a stage of the 1997 PruTour, the forerunner of the Tour of Britain, during the final kilometres of a stage into Swindon, routed over the notorious 'Magic Roundabout', a bewildering series of mini roundabouts orbiting a central roundabout. The *peloton*, numbering some 128 riders upon entry to the roundabout, was, within seconds, shattered into fourteen distinct lines, as riders tried to pick the correct path through the road furniture.

In the end, only the German Tour de France winner Jan Ullrich managed by chance to stay on the intended race route, even though he had been detached from the *peloton* by some ten minutes, and coasted in alone, to the wild celebration of the crowd. Ullrich himself seemed nonplussed by the victory, and scarcely looked up at the finishing line, as he was concentrating hard on sending a text message on his new team-issue T-Mobile phone to congratulate his mother on her fifty-fifth birthday.

Prolo *nmf*

Short for 'prologue'. A 'pleb' or 'prole'.

Often used to describe a rider, like Britain's Chris Boardman, who shamelessly specialised in winning the opening short prologue of the Tour de France, to the exclusion of any other stages, in a flagrantly undisguised bid to wear the yellow jersey on the podium of the first day, before relinquishing it the following day without any sense of regret. Embarrassing, really.

Prométhée *nm*

A rider who, like the mythical Prometheus whose liver was pecked out daily by an eagle only to grow back overnight, is capable of featuring in successive breakaways on consecutive stages of Grand Tours.

Not to be confused with the tragic story of Charly Prat, whose liver was actually pecked out by an eagle after a fall on the descent of the Tourmalet in the 1907 Tour de France. Sadly for Prat, it never grew back. He was disqualified by the *commissaire*.

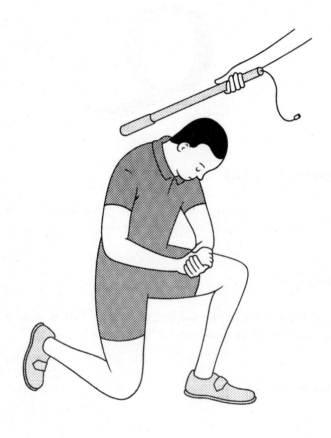

Queen *nm*

A British rider with a title.

Quadrangulaire *adj*

Slow. A bad day in the saddle can be described as *quadrangulaire*, as if the wheels of one's bike were square.

Quadrupède *adj*

Fast. A good day in the saddle can be described as *quadrupède*, as if one were pedalling one's bike with four feet.

Quantique *adj*

Quantum.

Descriptive of any sudden, organic and inexplicable movement from within the *peloton*, be it a funnelling, stretching out or sudden fattening of the bunch, that appears to have no causal origin and to serve no discernible purpose.

Québécois *adj*

Faux French. Not French. Sounds a bit French, but isn't really.

Natives of the actual Republic, generally speaking, look down on anything that claims to have what it considers to be dubious French heritage. This dismissive attitude is particularly applicable when it comes to riders from countries like the United States and the UK, who relocate to the south of France.

These exiles from the English-speaking world often become overly fixated with adopting a French persona, growing affected stubble, listening to dreadful French rock, pretending to know the difference between a Nuits-Saint-Georges and a Gigondas and marrying an actual French woman.

Some of these Anglophone blow-ins will even go as far, in their bid for adopted Frenchness, as signing for an actual French team like Cofidis and entering an endless stream of quaint and uncompetitive French races like the Circuit des Landes.

But, like the citizens of Quebec, they'll be destined forever to be suffering from a split identity, shunned by both their hosts and the old country they left behind.

Quiche *nf*

A half-baked breakaway; one which looks good enough from a distance, but which might just crumble apart at the first sting of pressure.

Quiconque *pron*

Whoever. (See *Jérôme.*)

A rider of such interchangeable anonymity that no one, neither fans, commentators nor fellow riders, can be bothered correctly to identify them. Instead, the cycling world damns them into invisibility by simply referring to them using the name of the team they ride for, and the prefix 'the rider from . . .'

It was Jacques Anquetil, the famously haughty five-time Tour de France winner, who first used the phrase, in reference to Raymond Poulidor, who finished second to him on roughly 937 occasions.

Rambo *nm*

A rider who is kidding himself he's still twenty-two.

R

Rat *nm*

A sneaky, devious rider.

Ratière *nf*

A trap into which sneaky, devious riders willingly fall.

Most common among these rat traps are stage finishes with hidden climbs in the final kilometre, tucked away and out of sight, just behind a left-handed bend. Such difficult ramps in the final few hundred metres are normally enough to stop any rider who has snuck off from the front of the *peloton*, in a flagrant attempt to upset the natural order of things, and deny the bigger names their chance of winning.

In recent times, the finish of Stage One of the 2014 Tour de France in Harrogate, Yorkshire was just such a *ratière*. The design of the final push uphill to the finish line was carefully calibrated to result in the *rats* getting caught directly outside

Bettys Tea Rooms, where reservations at tables by the window had been changing hands for several thousand pounds.

Ration *nf*

A rider with a small amount of *rat* about him.

Just enough to be considered admirably full of guile, without attracting the unwanted reputation for being sneaky and devious.

Rattachement *nm*

The reassimilation into the bunch of a *rat* after a sneaky, devious attack.

Ravageur *nm*

One who lays waste to a hotel room, ferreting away every sachet of shower gel, complimentary biscuit, free bottle of water and even the little sewing kit.

A *ravageur* often has the same attitude to food and drink handed to him during a race, preferring, instead of consuming them as intended, to horde the energy gels for later, and trying to wangle as many 'freebies' from the team car as possible.

Reptilien *adj*

This is a different order of animalistic behaviour on a bike. It is the kind of behaviour that wins races in unexpectedly savage ways (see *Crocodile*).

A *coureur reptilien* is a cold-blooded rider, often from southern Spain, who only really gets up to racing speed when the thermometer is touching 40°C, akin to a lizard emerging into the morning sunshine to gain body heat.

No one figure from the past encapsulates this epithet more fulsomely than the wildly dislikeable Alfonso Del Bosque, the veteran winner of the Pyrenean Queen Stage of the 1949 Tour de France. He was famous not only for his unspeakable arrogance, but also for his ruthlessness, born from a long and bloody campaign as one of General Franco's key lieutenants during the Spanish Civil War.

The stage of the Tour de France that he won was marred by the fatal collapse of his teammate Oscar Ibanez on the Hautacam. Ibanez had been in a breakaway all day, until he fell off the pace, and collapsed through heat exhaustion alone on a remote stretch of road. Del Bosque, who had attacked the group of favourites, rode across to where his friend lay by the side of the road, and, according to a local shepherd who happened to be the only eyewitness to the incident, robbed his teammate's prone corpse of a chocolate bar, a pork sausage and all his remaining water, before leaving him, literally, for dead, and riding to victory.

Del Bosque never confessed to his alleged actions, nor ever spoke publicly about what had happened that sweltering day on the slopes of the Hautacam. But many scholars of the sport have drawn conclusions about the possible sense of guilt that may have tormented Del Bosque in later life, from the posthumous publication of a surprisingly frank book of nursery rhymes titled *The Reptile of the Pyrenees*.

Del Bosque came to a mysterious end in 1971. He was found dead on the Hautacam, his pockets stuffed with chocolate bars and a pork sausage clenched between his teeth.

Rhabillage *nm*

The act of getting dressed all over again.

Changeable weather in early summer, and on mountain stages with considerable altitude gain and loss, can often become a series of tiresome wardrobe changes. Pulling on and off rain jackets and gloves is easier said than done on a bike. Some excel at it, while others fail miserably.

The uncontested *maître de rhabillage* was the young Parisian climber Florian Bouchon, a notable fashionista and sometime jazz flautist of the early 1970s. His constant pulling on and taking off of clothing throughout a race didn't stop with gilets and rain capes. He would often accessorise his outfits with the addition of a simple flower in his buttonhole, or indeed the addition of a buttonhole in the first place. He favoured black lace gloves, with which from time to time he fanned himself on hotter days. He also liked to restyle his hair every 10 kilometres, and carried an aerosol hairspray in his second bottle cage, confusing TV commentators of the epoch by the constant realignment of his side parting (this was before the mandatory wearing of helmets was introduced, but when side partings were compulsory).

Risque-tout *nmf*

Participation in an autumnal *lèchefrite* in some far-flung part of the globe (China) in a desperate bid to get a win, any win.

The reward to jeopardy ratio is alarming. A stage victory in, for example, the Tour of the Wuxi Industrial Development Basin may enable a rider who is out of contract to bluff his way into a new deal with a second-tier Dutch outfit. But a series of chastening failures against the mediocre opposition of which such a race is constituted (normally featuring such teams as the Hong Kong Combined Botanical Sciences Students CC, Think Australia Drink Australia and the Taiwanese champions Go Go Mini Pants) might just spell the end of an entire career.

Rivetage *nm*

The incremental ramping up of the pace in a bike race, until, almost imperceptibly, every rider is forced forward onto their saddle, perching 'on the rivet'.

This term traditionally dates back to the era of handmade leather saddles whose thick hides were held into place by glistening copper rivets. These days, of course, such saddles are no longer used. But the word *rivetage* still persists in the *peloton*.

Among the French, Belgian and Italian teams its meaning remains unchanged.

However, it is now commonly used in the English-speaking cycling world to describe the greedy, binge consumption of box sets of American TV series on laptops in hotel rooms after dinner. If a rider comes down to breakfast with conspicuous bags under their eyes, they will often attribute this to a regrettable bout of *rivetage* the previous night ('I started on series four of *Breaking Bad*, and the next thing I knew it was Tuesday').

Rodéo *nm*

Ill-fated but highly amusing participation in a turbulent race over cobblestones.

Generally, this is understood to apply more directly to American riders, especially those from southern states, who are noticeably inept at staying upright on the *pavés* because every road in their native country is a perfectly smooth seven-lane highway. As a result of their lack of respect for the cobbles, a *rodéo* will invariably result in being thrown into the irrigation ditch by the side of the road in the introductory ten or fifteen metres of the first of a series of twenty-seven cobbled sectors. This is greeted with whoops of delight by the European *peloton*.

Rognon *nm*

A legitimate reason to withdraw from a bike race. A bona fide complaint, whose severity and veracity no one can doubt.

This phrase is derived from Eddy Merckx's abandoning of the 1975 Tour de France, after succumbing to kidney (*rognon*) poisoning, resulting from the punch to the lower back he suffered at the hands of a member of the public on the Puy de Dôme. In appalling distress, he climbed off the following day.

More recent *rognons* have included Jasper Bloemveld's withdrawal from the 1983 Tour after a team car ran over both his legs as he lay on the ground having crashed on a descent. The car's driver, having noticed the double 'bump' underneath his wheels, then compounded the matter by reversing back to the stricken rider, and doing it again, but backwards. Thankfully Bloemveld recovered.

He now runs a series of Life Coaching Spiritual Healing courses in Greenland for financial services executives, at which participants suspend themselves by the nipples like Richard Harris in *A Man Called Horse*. When they are taken down, they then lie in rows, while Bloemveld drives a quad bike back and forth across their legs.

Ten years later, in one of the most celebrated *rognons* of the modern era, a tearful Patrice Solitaire climbed off on Alpe d'Huez after news was relayed to him that his bungalow in the mining district of Lens had fallen into a sinkhole.

And in 2016, Cornish climber Davey Lee was forced to abandon a stage of the Tour de Suisse after inhaling a whole songbird on the climb up the Rettenbach glacier.

Rouleur *nm*

(i) Not a climber, or a sprinter, or a time-triallist. The magnolia of the *peloton*'s colour palate.
(ii) A British cycling fan in his late forties, often employed in corporate law, who has invested heavily in Merino wool and claims to appreciate artisan hand-smelted steel lugs.

Rumsteck *nm*

A fiction. One of many Tour de France myths that only the gullible believe.

Rump steak was, of course, widely believed to be the traditional method of padding one's shorts before the advent of proper cycling kits. It was often said that riders would then remove the meat from their underwear at the end of the stage, and order the chef to fry it up for their evening meal.

This was however, though oft repeated, utter nonsense, and gave rise to the expression 'to tell *un rumsteck*'.

The truth was actually considerably stranger. Early Tour riders would ensure that they travelled with a supply of rabbits, which they could cull, de-bone, dry and insert, fur still soft, into their shorts. Being rabbits, this method also had the advantage of producing a constant supply of replacement protection for longer races.

Samovar *nm*

A bubbling, seethingly hot *peloton*, labouring up a
climb in high summer, from the base of which riders
are occasionally dribbled, as if a tap were being opened,
and a small amount of professional cyclist escapes.

S

Sabbatique *adj*

Lacking in competitiveness for a (normally) short, if unspecified length of time.

Dirk Klijker, the Flemish winner of the 1911 edition of the Tour de France, is still acknowledged to have been responsible for the longest recorded *sabbatique* spell in anyone's racing career, spanning some twenty-two years. He made not the slightest mark on any race of any note for over two decades, finishing in the low hundreds every time, until suddenly taking the 1933 Tour by storm, at the age of forty-four.

When asked about this crushing victory, in light of his lack of form stretching back to a point three years before the outbreak of the First World War, he replied, with extraordinary candour, that this might best be explained by the 'vast quantity of cocaine with which I have most diligently prepared for every stage of this great race. It benefits not man to live for but a single day bereft of the majesty of this elixir, the snow of the Gods.'

Sanglier *nm*

A wild boar.

A German, Luxembourgish or Polish rider who is suddenly called into ruthless, violent action every time the race passes through a section of dense, dark forestry, but is cowed into obeisance for the duration of all urban races, exposed mountaintops, windy moorland or sun-kissed coastal routes.

Sans *prep*

Without.

To ride *sans* used to be considered unprofessional, and would often result in highly amusing pranks being played on riders who indulged in such abstinence, such as cling film being stretched over the toilet pan in their hotel rooms.

Savonnage *nm*

Soaping or lathering as a precursor to shaving. Preparing oneself for the profession of bike racing.

The ritual shaving of legs carries spiritual heft. It is a rite of passage, approached with solemnity, through which every junior must pass as they enter the professional ranks. And in a metaphorical sense, the gradual acquisition of racing experience is akin to the preparation of the surface of the skin before the application of the razor blade.

In 2008, during his work as a TV commentator, the late Laurent Fignon famously complained that the modern generation of French professional cyclists fell so visibly short of the acceptable standard because, in his words, 'they had not lathered up sufficiently. They are hacking at dry skin, so to speak. In my day it was understood that it was the *savonnage* that makes the rider. These kids think they can wield the blade straight from the cradle? They do not understand such power, such responsibility. No wonder they are covered in cuts and slashes.'

Scrotum *nm*

An extremely ugly and sensitive, but nevertheless very important, part of a race.

Sédatif *nm*

A far from affectionate nickname for the annual presentation of the route of the Tour de France.

It is an openly expressed dread among prominent riders, who are expected to attend the long-winded event at the Palais des Congrès in Paris, featuring interminable speeches by local dignitaries.

In fact, it rather took the edge off Bradley Wiggins's victory celebrations in Paris in 2012, when he realised, almost immediately, that, as a consequence of having won the Tour de France, he'd be forced to sit through the ceremonial presentation for the following year's route.

Serrurerie *nf*

The art of locksmithing. Understood within the francophone *peloton* to be a reference to the almost Masonic secrecy of French cycling culture.

The term *serrurerie* has become a by-word for complete immersion in the esoteric, hidden customs of the French racing cyclist. Indeed, the word itself presents so many difficulties in pronunciation to the non-French speaker (any French word made up of the letter 'r' to 40 per cent or more is deemed by most linguists to be unfeasibly French), that it serves on its own as a kind of lock, to which only native speakers have the key.

Serviette *nf*

A hastily devised, but nonetheless brilliant, tactical plan, drawn up on the back of a napkin over breakfast (see *Hiéroglyphe*).

Soigneur *nm*

Baldrick from *Blackadder*.

Soufflage *nm*

Blowing hard, but unconvincingly, leading to the conclusion that it is all for show. Bluffing.

Souricière *nf*

A mousetrap. A three-man breakaway on flat terrain, comprising two hefty Dutch puncheurs and one diminutive Basque climber. Not to be confused with other ill-balanced breakaways (see *Piège à éléphant*).

Spécial *nm*

An oddity, a unique rider, an outsider. The Special One.

The most celebrated *spécial* of modern times was the Uzbek sprinter Ruslan Ablamatov, who had been reared, so it was claimed, on the scrubland surrounding a defunct Soviet missile silo in the Karakalpakstan region, close to the Uzbek border.

His father Vitaly, a decorated Red Army major who disappeared shortly after the Moscow Olympics, had ended up living in the silo where he raised his son in a makeshift wigwam erected inside the abandoned missile control centre.

Brought up by his taciturn father (the identity of Ablamatov's mother was never established), who continued to guard the silo against enemy aggressors, the young Ablamatov grew increasingly restless. While his father kept watch for endlessly long shifts, Ruslan roamed further and further from 'home', exploring the semi-arid plains that stretched to the horizon, until one day he disappeared altogether. For more than seven years he was lost to the world.

One day, in early summer 1993, he resurfaced, riding a rusting Raleigh Chopper into the outskirts of the town of Muynak, accompanied by a pack of wild dogs. When the local police were called, the dogs withdrew into the steppe, snarling, and Ablamatov was taken off for questioning.

He revealed next to nothing about his missing years, even when interrogated by the same team of experts in Moscow who had deciphered the strange howling language of the 'Wolfgirl of Kropotkin'. Though he retained language from his early childhood, his vocabulary was restricted to 'only about eleven words, most of which related in some way to bicycle racing'. Ablamatov remained something of a mystery.

An arthouse documentary was made by the St Petersburg Institute of Fine Arts about his rehabilitation, and it briefly found favour with Moscow's emerging post-Glasnost intelligentsia. It featured repeated close-up footage of Ablamatov's teeth, intercut with shots from an early edition of Paris–Roubaix, set to a soundtrack from The Pixies. Two years later his case was featured in the United Kingdom in an episode of Channel Five's *Famous Freaks*.

But it wasn't until Ablamatov underwent a series of physiological tests at the Moscow Sports Academy that his obvious talent for cycling became apparent. Tested on the Krylatskoye track, he rode three times around the 333-metre circuit, banking at lightning speed, breaking all records, before abruptly leaving down the ramp, riding his bike along the corridor and out of the building.

For a further period of seven years, he disappeared without trace.

The next anyone saw of him was at a low-key press conference in the South of France. In 2011 he signed for Marseille La Pomme, and won the Grande Trophée d'Armagnac in his first season.

In 2013, after his son made his debut in the Tour de France, a dishevelled and tearful Vitaly Ablamatov was arrested in Tashkent where he had presented himself at the French Embassy demanding to be flown that night by helicopter to Pau. He was eventually convicted of attempting to smuggle meat products and failure to pay parking fines dating back twenty years.

Ruslan Ablamatov continues to ride for Lampre-Merida, and recently won a stage of the Tour of Britain into Stoke-on-Trent.

Sultan *nm*

The de facto chief of the *peloton* (see *Astronaute*). Often surrounded by a large number of affiliated supporting riders (see *Harem*).

Super *adj*

Very.

Thé *nm*

4 pm. It is widely understood that no British rider will attack for the following half hour.

T

Tambourinaire *nmf*

The least talented member of a squad, whose very presence is deemed by most to be largely decorous, like the tambourine player in a rock band (see *Bassiste*).

Tannerie *nf*

A race day of extremes in weather conditions: sunshine, rain, wind.

All of these elements affecting the race in swift succession can leave a rider's face looking, and feeling, like a well-worn leather saddle, cured and treated till it thickens into a tough hide surface.

The impression of weathered mania is then completed with vacant staring eyes embedded into the carcass of the face like the empty roundels of the polished brass rivets.

Tartare *adj*

Raw, battered-looking flesh, often served with an accompaniment of vile fluids of differing hues and textures as well as small, very sour body parts which resemble cocktail onions. The aftermath of a particularly unpleasant crash (see *Picasso* and *Nœud*).

Tartre *nm*

A build-up of matter around the delicate workings of the derailleur and the chain, which, left untreated, will cause decay. Not that this would bother a *gâcheur* in the slightest.

Taxidermie *nf*

Choosing to race the Tour de France, making yourself liable to declaring your earnings over three weeks to the French Inland Revenue. This is specific to Monaco-based members of the professional *peloton* (see *Corniche*).

Télé *nf abbrev*

Telly.

A crucially important waypoint on a race, as significant as a feed station, King of the Mountains points and intermediate sprints, the *télé* marker (or zone, as you can never be certain where exactly it will begin) denotes the estimated start of live TV coverage, and a signal for everyone to begin showing off wildly.

Variations of such extrovert behaviour include relaxed banter between riders of the same nationality on different teams, a serious-looking conversation over team radio, a thumbs-up to the camera, ostentatious consumption of small slices of cakes wrapped in tin foil, a brief sticking out of the tongue (followed by a winning smile), an irritable waving away of the camera bike and the iconic hand drawn across the throat – the universal sign that reads, 'I'm cooked'.

Téléenseignement *nm*

A term for distance learning, like the Open University with its weird programmes on BBC2. Only in cycling this is completely normal.

Since most teams only get their riders all together once or twice a year, and only so that they can try their new kit on and pose awkwardly as a group in front of a fork-lift truck or a giant shampoo bottle, almost all of a rider's 'training' is done remotely from the rider's home.

More enlightened, better funded teams, like Team Sky (see *Ciel*), have implanted sensors in the tissue of their riders' hearts, wirelessly connected by Bluetooth to a microchip in the palm of their hands, which is swiped each time they reach for their kettle and has been specially adapted to upload their biometric information straight to the team's subterranean headquarters built into the side of a volcano on Tenerife.

More normally, riders from other teams simply write down the number of kilometres they rode that day in their team-issue 'Cycling Journal', and get their parents to sign it.

Télégraphie *nf*

The art of riding quickly up the Col du Télégraphe, to the curious exclusion of any other climb.

Riders who excel at this very specific 11.8-kilometre climb are often, mysteriously, found wanting at other climbs, most notably the Col du Galibier (see *Galbé*), which normally follows immediately afterwards.

NB. In Surrey, in the United Kingdom, there is a similar phenomenon, albeit on a smaller scale, called 'Boxhillia'.

Télépathe *nmf*

A rider who so dislikes giving TV interviews that he will go out of his way to avoid them, even if this means threatening to chop the head off the journalist in question or stealing his/her microphone (see *Téléphone*).

Téléphone *nmf*

In many ways the opposite of a *télépathe*.

A *téléphone* speaks the language of *télé*, providing answers of sufficient brevity to be digestible into a perfectly formed fifteen-second soundbite (the optimum duration for a TV show) but with sufficient outspoken charm/humour/ controversy/hyperbole to be considered 'good value' for broadcast.

Great *téléphones* of recent years include Geraint Thomas, who can invariably be relied upon to sum up an assault on, say, Alpe d'Huez by describing it as, 'Pretty gnarly really. Like riding your pushbike up a bloody big mountain full of drunks. Like Caerphilly on a Friday night.'

Not to be confused with *jaillir*.

Télésiège *nm*

A chairlift in an Alpine resort. The mechanism by which a reasonably average climber is made to look better than they actually are on climbs by the presence of a team packed with mountain domestiques, most of whom are actually better than their leader, but have to pretend they aren't, because their leader is also the team owner's son.

Can also refer to armchair critics, or those who take a seat (*siège*) in front of the telly (*télé*).

Télex *nm*

A French cycling team, so called because telex machines were, until very recently, still the most common way that French teams would communicate with their riders.

Thermos *nm*

A climb of such length and intensity that, no matter how cold the ambient air might be, one's body temperature on the ascent will remain close to boiling point.

It should be noted, however, that in just the same way a thermos loses heat quickly once the lid has been unscrewed, so too will the rider rapidly cool down once he has reached the top and taken off his helmet.

Tilda *nf*

A rider such as Alejandro Valverde, who divides opinion, like Tilda Swinton does.

Timbalier *nm*

A timpanist. A rider whose job is so rarefied, and its application so rare, that he might as well be invisible save for the one specific moment when he is suddenly called into action (see *Niche*).

Gerd Keuken was just one such. The Flemish one-day specialist had grown up as the son of a Belgian signal master on a remote stretch of regional train track near Antwerp. As a result of a childhood spent peering out of his first-floor bedroom window at the passage of locomotives over the level crossing, whose barriers his father controlled, he developed a peculiar talent that he was able to put to use in later life.

He became famous throughout the *peloton* for being an expert in judging when it is safe to cross railways lines. His unerring instinct for getting his team to the front just in time for the first nine riders, all his teammates, to duck under the falling barriers, leaving the rest of the *peloton* stranded by the 15:27 to Ghent, was a highly prized asset in the Belgian classics season. His reading of the railway network and shepherding of the riders over the flat terrain, criss-crossed by train lines, was widely and directly credited with resulting in three Paris–Roubaix victories, two Tours of Flanders and a Scheldeprijs.

As such, his reputation as cycling's greatest ever *timbalier* is only really rivalled by Patrick Forsdyke, the Scottish naturalist who could read the signs of migrating wildfowl for sudden changes in atmospheric conditions during late-season one-day races in northern France.

Tisseur *nm*

A weaver. An ill-disciplined sprinter, who chops and changes his line in the final few hundred metres of a sprint, 'weaving' from side to side.

The act of weaving, or *tissage*, is considered to be one of cycling's worst breaches of etiquette, as it endangers everyone, not least the perpetrator. *Tisseurs* will be shunned, not only by members of rival teams, but even by their teammates. They will be reminded of their transgressions by riders visibly veering from side to side upon sight of them, even if the encounter takes place somewhere as innocuous as the breakfast buffet. Their colleagues will lurch violently, spilling milk from their cornflakes bowls, sometimes targeting the 'accidental' spill onto the lap of the perceived offender. Even the team's bus drivers will sometimes get in on the act, suddenly wrenching their steering wheel to guide the vehicle into three lanes of oncoming traffic on their way to the stage start. To make a point.

It is not common for *tisseurs* to persist in their behaviour.

Toison *nf*

Un toison d'or, or golden fleece, is the name given to a lucrative, if fleeting, appearance in the yellow jersey during the Tour de France (see *Bakélite*).

Even if the jersey is worn for one day only, after a breakaway succeeds against the odds but before the main Tour contenders choose to wipe out the advantage of the fortunate soul in the race lead, the very fact that the rider will forever be able to claim that he led the Tour de France opens up almost limitless (if largely cycling-based) opportunities to make a living in their retirement. This phenomenon is known as 'wearing the golden fleece'.

Sylvain Jarre, wearer of the yellow jersey for one day on the 1997 Tour, and who retired in 2005, established a chain of garden centres in the Dordogne, known as Jarre's Jardins Jaunes, which exclusively stocked yellow-flowering plants.

Ten years prior to that, Thierry Maréchal found himself in the national spotlight as the leader of the Tour. His unfancied Babybel Fromages team unexpectedly won the team time trial on Stage Four of the 1987 Tour, when a thunderstorm broke immediately after they crossed the line, hampering the chances of all the remaining teams.

As a result, he too found unexpected ways to monetise his moment of cycling glory. In fact, even before the race had reached Paris, he had released a number one hit, entitled 'La Vie en Jaune', recorded in a makeshift studio on the second rest day in Avignon. 'La Vie en Jaune' was only knocked off the top spot by Vanessa Paradis's 'Joe le Taxi'. Maréchal is now a judge on the French TV version of *The Voice*.

Tricéphale *adj*

Three-headed. A team with multiple leaders.

The Armani Fagotti team of the mid 1990s will long be remembered for the chaotic power struggle that character-ised its three participations in the Tour de France. Three cousins, all related through the Milanese industrialist Fagotti family, who manufactured tableware, vied increasingly bit-terly for pre-eminence within the team.

Although subsequently aped by the T-Mobile team of Jan Ullrich, Andreas Klöden and Alexander Vinokourov, they are still accepted as having set the benchmark. The Fagottis were the ultimate *équipe tricéphale*, and their internecine feuding was a source of great amusement in the French boulevard press.

The opening salvo was fired by the eldest of the cousins, Marco Fagotti, embroidering military-style epaulettes onto his racing jersey as a statement of his senior rank. This was countered by cousin Paolo's insistence on being piped on board the team bus at the start of stages. But it was the youngest of the three cousins, Giovanni, who won this particular battle, when he managed to persuade the remaining six team members to lock both Paolo and Marco in the chemical toilet on board. Had they not been freed just in time by a concerned passer-by who heard frantic banging and screaming coming from within the Armani Fagotti team bus, they might have missed the sign-on and been ejected from the race.

By a curious quirk of fate, the three cousins finished in 126th, 127th and 128th place.

Usufruitier *adj obs*

Usufructuary. (Rarely used in modern cycling.)

U

Unijambiste *nmf*

An unbalanced, awkward-seeming cycling stylist.

Gianni Baldo, who came to cycling late (having previously run an eel farm near Lake Como), and whose career blossomed in the early 1970s when he twice finished runner-up to Eddy Merckx in the green jersey points competition, was widely considered to be the most ungainly rider ever to have ridden the Tour.

Video footage of the time will attest to his propensity for lurching violently to the right with each downward stroke of his left foot (his legs were eight centimetres different in length), and his head pivoted suddenly to the left and back to the centre, as if he were swimming front crawl. He also gasped for air with each pedal turn, and emitted a continual groan, like the drone of a meditating Buddhist monk. His elbows were crooked at an awkward angle in a style that has recently become known as *à la Froome*.

After the 1973 Tour, the French toy manufacturer Roullet & Decamps produced a special-edition 'Baldo le Bouffon' doll, which proved to be very popular. The doll was articulated so that its joints were poorly aligned and loosely connected. And of course, one leg was much longer than the other.

Urologie *nf*

The theory, study and practice of eluding the anti-doping authorities.

Urologue *nmf*

A master practitioner of *urologie*.

This is often a rider in possession of an attaché case stuffed with elaborate tubing, unsettlingly lifelike prosthetic penises, improvised whoopee cushions converted to act as bladders, hernia trusses, and litres of pristine, blameless urine (see *Eau bénite*) harvested from their children's kindergarten in Girona.

Uruguayen *adj*

Any rider of indeterminate, yet probably South American, origin, who isn't a *colombien*.

Utérus *nm*

The 'pregnant' state of a swollen, almost complete *peloton* on the initial slopes of a climb, before riders are 'born' of the back (see *Samovar*).

The legendary German domestique Jens Voigt once described the agony of holding on before being dropped from an ever-thinning *peloton* on the Galibier as, 'The bunch was like a giant womb. It was really horrible, the closest thing us guys with our hairy chins and balls will ever know to the pain of giving birth. And my wife's had six kids. Imagine that! I must be a right bastard to make her go through that six times. But I was only following Chris Boardman's example. He's, like, totally my hero.'

Voigt rode the Tour de France fifty-two times before retiring in 2022.

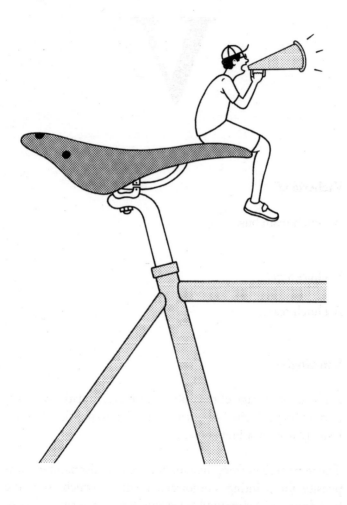

Vespa *nf*

A laughably small and surprisingly noisy Italian rider.

V

Vacherie *nf*

A Dutch team bus.

Vachers *nmpl*

A Dutch team.

Van Gogh *nm*

A transitional stage of the Tour de France. A relatively unimportant day's racing of great beauty, but no significance. Usually won by a Frenchman.

The term derives from the Dutch Expressionist painter's propensity for painting sunflowers, fields of which form the backdrop and foreground for overly long, lingering shots of the *peloton* trundling along for hour after hour of inconsequential television coverage.

Consequently, a piffling, minor victory on such an unimportant and weakly contested stage is known as *une victoire de Van Gogh*.

The unfortunate winner will often be ridiculed by the rest of the *peloton* the following day, when riders will come up alongside the unfortunate cyclist and bellow their faux congratulations into his left ear, in reference to the self-mutilation carried out by the Dutch master.

Vatican *nm*

An Italian team bus.

Vaticiner *vi*

To make unduly bold predictions about what one might go on to achieve (see also *Minimiser*).

There are only so many times one can reasonably be expected to fall short of one's grand pronouncements, before one has to deliver on the promise, as flamboyant American time-triallist Larry Hinkelstein discovered to his cost in 1984.

When he declared, for the eleventh consecutive day, that he would 'kick [Laurent] Fignon's yellow-chickin, cotton-pickin', burger-flippin' French ass all around the Eiffel Tower', the cycling world still sat up and took notice. But Hinkelstein was deluded. As Fignon placed second on a summit finish that afternoon, the American came in fifty-eight minutes later in 162nd. In the individual time trial the following day, he fared still worse, trailing in 186th. He abandoned on Stage Thirteen, citing illness and declaring that 'Fignon must think Thanksgiving's come early this year. So let him eat all the turkey he wants, but I'll tell y'all this much: Old Hinky'll be back next year to teach that cheese-munchin', wine-guzzlin', onion-carryin' . . .' (etc).

In fact, Fignon, when interviewed about Hinkelstein on the twentieth anniversary of his second victorious Tour in 1984, claimed never to have heard of him, nor the Lucky Strike team he professed to have ridden for.

Fignon, for the record, won two Tours de France.

Hinkelstein, when last tracked down by journalist William Fotheringham for his book *Enfant Salaud! The Tour's Biggest Dickheads*, runs a small franchise of Dunkin' Donuts in Winnfield, Louisiana.

Verrier *nm*

A glassworker. A rider who treats his equipment with such delicacy that he never appears to want to put it under any strain, lest it shatter.

A polite way of implying his utter lack of effectiveness.

Vertige *nm*

The experience of a rider who is suddenly elevated to a standing that far exceeds his capacity. To use a term from football parlance, he is suffering from a 'nosebleed' as a result of the altitude at which he unaccustomedly finds himself operating.

The phrase was coined by the popular press after the infamous Tour of 1922, the first, and so far only, yellow jersey for the Island of Curaçao. It was Randal Kross, the son of a Dutch lighthouse-man from Santa Catarina, who found himself with a staggering one hour, twenty-two minute lead over the Belgian favourite Firmin Lambot going into the final 240-kilometre stage from Dunkirk to Paris, courtesy of a catastrophic wrong turning taken by everyone except for Kross the previous day (see *Prisme*).

The rider from Curaçao had been so far off the back that he failed to take the same wrong turning as the rest, and ended up following the correct signage that had been adjusted by the organisation after they realised their mistake. The bunch had laboured for 60 kilometres due west into a headwind, before seeing the error of their ways and turning round towards the finish line in Dunkirk. Meanwhile Kross was taking the win.

But, despite his tremendous advantage, the pressure got to the young Curaçaon, especially when he confessed to having suffered from vertigo as a child, an affliction that had marred his early years, exacerbated when his father had sent him up a ladder to clean the outside of the lighthouse.

The psychological frailty associated with Kross's sense of *vertige* was widely suspected to have led to his complete collapse on the approach to Paris. He trailed in some three hours down on the rest of the field, largely forgotten by the race, and with the finish-line grandstand being dismantled around him.

Competing theories, however, suggest that his sudden loss of form might not have been purely down to his perceived condition of *vertige*. His almost inexplicable race-losing capitulation might have been more directly attributable to his abduction near the Belgian border and subsequent detention in a carpet factory at the hands of Flemish cycling fans, who only released him after three hours.

Vinokourov *adj*

Worthy of, certain to provoke, or resulting in total disbelief.

Viscosité *nf*

A certain slowness of tactical thought during the heat of the battle in a bike race, associated with riders who are estimably muscled, but not widely read.

Vivre *vi*

To live. A word used by professional cyclists to describe the daily occupation of all those who do not ride a bicycle for a living (see *Être* and *Faire*).

Vogue *nf*

Any passing fad, such as the wearing of life-affirming crystals as pendants in the late 1990s, often associated with a love for the music of Peter Gabriel.

Cycling has always been susceptible to bizarre ephemeral tendencies. It was, for example, widely believed in the inter-war years that the carrying of Polynesian totems helped in decision-making under extreme physical duress. Likewise, more recently, in the late 1980s, the application of almond-flavoured tincture behind the earlobes was a much-vaunted measure to combat fatigue.

At the same time, there was a counter-movement, orchestrated by a core of Swiss riders who argued vehemently against any use of nut oil, on the grounds that it could cause contact dermatitis. Their alternative method of combating the inevitable onset of tiredness during a race was simply to grow a ponytail.

These days every single rider routinely undergoes ornate and expensive body-art procedures whose bloodthirsty and arcane designs are believed to ward off attention from tax inspectors.

Vulcanisation *nf*

To rubberise. Often used when describing the black streaky markings on a road after a mass pile-up in the final kilometre. *Une grande vulcanisation* is to be avoided at all costs.

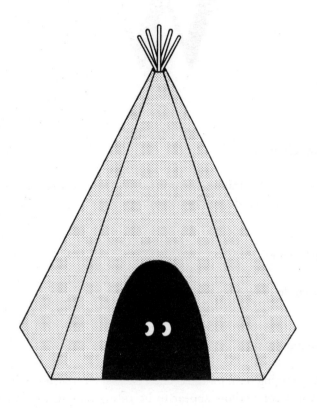

Wigwam *nm*

The awning erected alongside the Team Sky (see *Ciel*)
bus, under which Bradley Wiggins hides from the public.

Wagnérien *adj*

Relating to the dramatic ascension over the brow of a hill of
the fleet of Tour de France helicopters.

Walkyrie *nf*

A Tour de France helicopter pilot.

Water-polo *nm*

A disparaging term for the cycling element of triathlon races,
in which competitors appear to be riding only in the same
skimpy pair of Speedo trunks they used to go swimming,
more suited to team sports in the local municipal pool.

Week-end *nm*

A 'weekend' rider, *un coureur de week-end*, is widely revered, but seldom understood in professional cycling. He comes to life on Saturdays and Sundays, when race organisers generally schedule the hardest stages in order to maximise TV audiences. When the race gets easier again, he disappears back into anonymity.

Wiggins *nm*

Something that happens once.

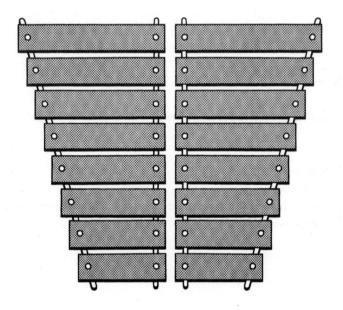

Xylophone *nm*

An overly skinny rider (see *Égouttoir).*

X

X *nm*

A flat stage (derived from the mathematical term 'x-axis').

Xavier *nm*

A rider who will only consider getting in a breakaway on a flat stage (see *X*).

Yates *nm*

The generic term for a British rider on the Tour.

Y *nm*

A mountain stage (derived from the mathematical term 'y-axis').

Yachtman *nm*

A rider whose inflated sense of self-worth leads them to apply for residency in Monaco, just in case someone wants to pay them €1,000,000 per annum (see *Corniche* and *Taxidermie*).

Yann *nm*

A rider who will only consider getting in a breakaway on a mountain stage (see *Y*).

Yaourt *nm*

Yoghurt. A minor, poorly funded race on the brink of extinction and staged in a remote region of France, such as La Drôme.

The term is derived from the lack of catering facilities available to the teams at the one-star accommodation booked by the organisers. That, in turn, leads to unavoidable dinner stops at motorway service stations en route to the following day's stage start. It is well known in the *peloton* that the selection of sandwiches available is so depressing that one tends to roam to and from the fridge area, consistently drawn to the fall-back option of a strawberry-flavoured yoghurt drink, in lieu of anything resembling a meal.

It is not uncommon, during the month of June, to witness entire teams of underweight, track-suited young men leaving a petrol station through the sliding glass doors, clutching white bottles of a dairy-based beverage known as Yop.

Yougoslavie *nf*

A short-lived team whose incarnation came about as the result of a succession of uncomfortable mergers.

Much like in the Balkan wars, the inevitable dissolution of a *yougoslavie* is often rancorous, setting friend against friend, and, in the case of Bennie and Bert Kloppers, brother against brother.

The Kloppers brothers, the twin sons of famous Dutch greyhound trainer Knut Kloppers, whose relationship had broken down over a dispute about gambling debts allegedly incurred at the Voorburg dog track near Amsterdam, unwillingly found themselves racing together when their respective teams

BigRibs and Aachener Auspuff merged to create the hybrid BigRibs-Auspuff team of 1993.

The two team sponsors, uneasy from the outset with the halved exposure resulting from the merger, pulled the plug definitively after the unedifying sight was broadcast of Bennie and Bert brawling outside a Grenoble multi-storey car park during the first rest day of the 1993 Tour de France. Bert was finally pulled off his twin brother by two of his former Auspuff teammates, leaving Bennie clutching a broken nose and hollering at his twin, 'Fucking BigRib loser!'

Yo-yo *nm*

An indefatigable but stupid rider, whose perpetual attempts to get in a breakaway are a source of genuine amusement in the *peloton*, watching him disappear into the distance, only to reach the invisible extent of his powers and start spinning backwards to the bunch.

Zeus *nm*

An overly bearded rider.

Z

Zébrer *vtr*

To ride in the middle of the road, eyes lowered, and in a state of virtual catatonia, induced by the flashing past of the white stripes on the tarmac.

Zoom *nm*

A distant second place. One that will only be visible to a camera with a very long lens.

Zut! *excl*

An exclamation of dismay at a frankly unsatisfactory ending.